Quiver^X

Children: God's Special Blessing

By Jim and Shannon French

This book is dedicated to:

Orrin, Cindy, and Chloe,
With all our love

May the Lord grant you the
desires of your heart!

Table of Contents

Introduction

The term "Quiver^x" is taken from Psalm 127:4-5: "As arrows [are] in the hand of a mighty man; so [are] children of the youth. Happy [is] the man that hath his quiver full of them: they shall not be ashamed, but they shall speak with their enemies in the gate." Over the last decade or so the term "quiver full" has come to be used in Christian circles in relation to a husband and wife who don't prevent conception but instead who choose to allow the Lord to give them as many children as He chooses in whatever timing He desires. We have taken this term "quiver full" and modified it. The "^{x}" hearkens back to our days in algebra class when "x" was the unknown number. Therefore, Quiver^x refers to the fact that we don't know how many children we will have in our quiver, and it indicates our willingness to find out by welcoming each child with an open heart.

This book is written to the church today. We hope that by outlining what the Lord has told us, we will challenge each couple to search the Scriptures and pray and ask the Lord what He would have them do in this area of their marriage. For too long the church has listened to the voice of our society on this subject rather than seeking Scriptural guidance. Let this information be food for thought, and if the Lord leads you down this path, let it also be encouragement and a resource for making your own journey fulfilling.

> 2 Timothy 1:7 — "For God has not given us a spirit of fear, but of power and of love and of a sound mind."

> 2 Timothy 3:16 — "All Scripture is given by inspiration of God, and is profitable for doctrine, for reproof, for correction, for instruction in righteousness."

CHAPTER 1

Why Quiver^x in America Today

Modern Molechs

"The Bible calls debt a curse and children a blessing. But in our culture, we apply for a curse and reject blessings. Something is wrong with this picture." - Doug Philips (Vision Forum)

Children are a blessing from the Lord, but in our culture we don't really view them as a blessing anymore. We view them as an inconvenience, like they are not worth the trouble or are too expensive.

For years my wife, Shannon, and I dreamed about all the cool things we could do as a couple and all the neat places that we would like to visit. Even though Shannon and I had a baby right out of the marriage chute, and I used to think that would be it. I thought, "We've had our obligatory child, now let's get this child raised and on its own quickly so we can get back to our married life, so we can save for our trip to the Holy Land or to Europe, so we can plan our next getaway at one of our favorite places, Cedar Point." It was really inconvenient trying to ride a roller coaster as a couple when we had a two-year-old in a stroller. We couldn't just say, "Excuse me sir" (to the 6'6" 250-pound man wearing a tank top and holding a stein full of beer), "would you please watch our daughter so we can ride the roller coaster together?" I learned early on as a parent that this type of action should not be carried out. God gives us our children for a reason. Ahh yes, but the question is, for what reason? What reason indeed? The Lord seeks a godly heritage from us, a righteous nation that will not falter in the face of enemy activity. He wants a generation that will rise up as a great heavenly steamroller and sweep through our nation and our world on a mission from God that will not fail.

In Leviticus 18, verse 21, the Word says, "And you shall not let any of your descendants pass through the fire to Molech, nor shall you profane the name of your God: I am the Lord." In those days the people sacrificed their children by fire. Today we are in many respects still sacrificing them, only now we do so by science and by artificial means. Please hear our hearts in this matter. We once used artificial methods to limit the number of children we would conceive, until a friend of mine showed some scriptures to me, which allowed God to open our hearts to the whole idea of letting Him do our family planning. In other words, we don't do anything to prohibit conception, either chemically/hormonally or by manipulating the timing of our physical relationship, and we personally feel an obligation to make sure that all of the plumbing is working, so to speak. Above and beyond that, my wife and I enjoy each other, and if the Lord chooses to give us another child, that is fine with us. I will be the first one to admit that we have never been faced with any health challenges in this lifestyle. I know people personally who have encountered many challenges, both real and perceived, that could interfere with their ability to remain Quiver[x]. We pray that we would remain true to our scriptural convictions even in the light of physically challenging circumstances, if we are ever faced with such a situation.

Our goal in this book is NOT to tell you what to do. Big surprise? I hope not. The truth is that no one really can "make" anyone do anything that they don't want to do. Our goal is to provide a scriptural basis for Quiver[x] and give you all of the "other stuff" that you may not know about the subject, presenting the information in a fresh, scriptural way, and also relating it to our culture today. When a husband and wife make the decision to serve the Lord with their whole heart, together, we want them to have this information as part of their knowledge base to draw from. We believe that each couple armed with knowledge of the truth and wisdom needs to seek the Lord in this area and make their decision based on the inner workings of the Holy Spirit. We hope this book will be a catalyst for couples to discuss the issue and seek the Lord together, so they will be in unity on this subject and be able to stand with a clear conscience before the Lord.

Keep in mind that the point of this book is not that you should have as many children as you can. The goal is not to have large families, although we acknowledge that a large family can often be the result. The point of this book is for each couple to seek the Lord's will together and in agreement yield their family planning to the Lord. We know families who have followed this principle and have no children or only one child so far. We know other families who have followed this principle and have a dozen or more children. We know families who have been called to adoption, either in addition to their biological children or instead of them. No family size is better than any other. A family with nine children is not any more sanctified than a family with one child, if that's what the Lord chooses to give them. It's about fulfilling what God wants for each of us. So regardless of the size of your family, or whether you have even had children, we encourage you to read through this book and spread the message of God's special blessing — children.

CHAPTER 2

The Law of First Mention
Right Out of the Birth Canal

"Six children are the minimum number for people of normal stock; those of better stock should have more!" -President Theodore Roosevelt, 1907[1]

What does God say right from the very beginning of Genesis chapter one? Let us delve into the Scriptures and see what the Lord has to say about having children. We believe that the Bible is not open to personal interpretation but that we should let the Bible interpret the Bible. I have personally read through the Bible many times and have taken most of my family through the whole Bible, although some of the younger children are just now hearing parts for the first time. As a godly Christian father, I want my children to get most of their Bible instruction from me. There are so many influences in the world, and I want to make sure they get the proper teaching from one of the major, God-ordained, proper sources – their father. However, you can't teach what you don't know, so it is of utmost importance to us as fathers to know the Word and be ready at all times to share a biblical lesson with our children or to be able to share a testimony of what the Lord has done for us in any situation.

Back to the "The law of first mention:" this means that where God conveys something to us for the very first time chronologically in the Bible, we had better sit up and take notice of the instruction, for it will lay the ground work for interpretation throughout the rest of the Bible. For those of you wanting a more formal definition, here it is:

> The law of first mention may be said to be *the principle that requires one to go to that portion of the Scriptures where a doctrine is mentioned for the first time and to study the first occurrence of the same in order to get the fundamental inherent meaning of that doctrine.* When we thus see the first appearance, which is usually in the simplest form, we can then examine the doctrine in other portions of the Word that were given later. We shall see that the fundamental concept in the first occurrence remains dominant as a rule, and colors all later additions to that doctrine.[2]

Applying the law of first mention to the subject of childbearing, we start in Genesis chapter 1, verses 27 and 28:

> "So God created man in His own image; in the image of God He created him; male and female He created them. Then God blessed them, and God said to them, Be fruitful and multiply; fill the earth and subdue it; have dominion over the fish of the sea, over the birds of the air, and over every living thing that moves on the earth."

The very first recorded event that transpired between God and His newly formed creation was for Adam and Eve to receive a blessing and then be given a charge. Verse 28 says that He blessed them. I don't know about you, but I love it when the Lord blesses me. I don't think I would ever tell someone, "No thanks, I've had enough blessings for now." So He blessed them and then told them to be fruitful and multiply, to fill the earth and subdue it. Now that seems fairly straightforward: to have children and lots of them, to fill the earth and subdue it. The Lord, in this "first mention" passage, is linking children with blessing.

This passage then sets the tone for the whole rest of the Bible and how God views our children. All of the plans for our children, all of our dreams for them, all of His divine fulfillment begins right here.

There are recorded instances in Scripture where the Lord purposely closed off someone's womb so that they could not have children, or when the Lord specifically opened someone's womb to allow them to have children. In Genesis 25:21 we read how Isaac prayed for Rebekah to have children, and how the Lord granted his plea so that Rebekah conceived twins. In Genesis 30:1-2, Rachel tells Jacob to "Give me children, or else I die!" Jacob responds in verse two by saying, "Am I in the place of God who has withheld ... the fruit of your womb?" Then in verse 30 God remembers Rachel and takes away her disgrace by giving her Joseph.

In Exodus Chapter 1 we read how Israel was growing its population by leaps and bounds, and this worried the king of Egypt. He instructed the midwives to kill all the male babies, but the midwives feared God more than they feared the king of Egypt, so they let the male babies live. The God-given purpose for children was so clear in the minds of the midwives that they willfully disobeyed the king of Egypt. They knew that God's plan and purpose was to raise up a new generation with a godly heritage, and there was no way that they were going to participate in the destructive plans of the enemy.

When Moses was born, they saw that he was a beautiful child and hid him for three months. I believe that they saw beyond the drool, messy diapers, and feeding every two hours. Hebrews 11:23 says that they were not afraid of the king's command. How many times are our reproductive choices motivated by a fear of something rather than by the Word of God? We may fear having a lack of support, finances, wisdom, or strength. The Word tells us that fear is not from God. "For God has not given us a spirit of fear, but of power and of love and of a sound mind" (2 Timothy 1:7). In all our decisions, fear should not be our motivating factor.

The preceding scriptures lay a solid foundation for interpreting what the Bible says about children and the womb; about how He wants to reward and bless us; and about how God wants to help us mature as a couple and as part of a Christian heritage linking arms with our brothers and sisters in the Lord to see His great purposes fulfilled in the land.

The threads of these biblical truths start in the very first chapter of the Bible and run consistently throughout the rest, as we will see as we delve into other details in other chapters of this book. We will also talk about more scriptures in the context of other subjects.

CHAPTER 3

Blessings of the Lord
From Family Frailties to Fullness, Famine to Feasts

"How can there be too many children? That's like saying there are too many flowers."
- Mother Teresa

Children are a reward from the Lord. I remember back to when I had my first child. I was scared out of my wits. I remember thinking that things must have been very different from the Lord's perspective for Him to call this child a reward and a blessing. I didn't know what to do. I didn't know how to take care of a baby. Every time I held her I was sure that I was bringing her imminent doom and that my nervous butterfingers would surely cost my child her life. I thought that she was some fragile creature who was barely able to sustain herself, and that the slightest breeze would bring her the plague. I used to think to myself, "Shouldn't we keep her in a plastic bubble until she's 21 or so?" Most assuredly I felt utterly incapable of doing anything for this child other than provide adequate financial support for her and my wife. So that is about all I did. I look back with deep regret at not being around more when my family was younger. I wish I could have spent much more time with both of them in the beginning of our journey.

It wouldn't be until about nine years later that a friend of mine talked to us about the idea of being "quiver full" and letting the Lord plan our children. He showed us many scriptures, and my wife and I spent a great deal of time in prayer on the subject. Eventually the Lord made it clear that this was the right thing to do. At one point I had been perfectly content to have my token one child for grandparents, raise her as quickly as possible, and get her out of the house as soon as possible so that my wife and I could get on with our marriage. I had a very skewed world-view on this subject. Now I can't imagine life without all six (soon to be seven) of my children, and I pray that the Lord will continue to bless me with more children. I don't want to look back with any more regret or be haunted by the two words – "what if?" Here is the key to having happy times. Are you ready for this? I know I wasn't and still am not in some respects since the scale needs to be adjusted every time I have more children. The key is to spend time with your children. This is time that I would have spent on myself, maybe not even necessarily in a bad activity, but time I controlled nonetheless. The amount of time that you have to spend on your own pursuits is directly related to the number of children you have.

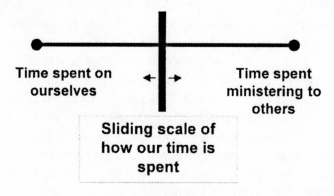

We either spend time on ourselves (and some time is necessary, obviously) or we spend time ministering to others. My slider was very far to the left, with the majority of my time being spent on myself. It has moved further to the right with each new child as I spend more time ministering to my children (and others). This is a good thing, since we gain greater Christian maturity as we decrease and He increases. But more on this in a later chapter when we discuss how we've short-sheeted ourselves as a culture and as the church. We've not attained the level of full Christian maturity that the Lord desires. And we haven't transferred the lessons learned in child rearing to evangelism and discipleship of others, which is the rearing of spiritual children.

Children who are being trained up properly truly are a blessing. They are a wonderful addition to what has become known as Team French. My oldest daughter is now one of the greatest blessings my wife and I could hope for. She is free from the normal (I think not-normal when trained properly) worries of teenage rebellion. She has so learned this lifestyle and increased her capacity for child rearing that when she has children it will be a relatively easy process for her, hopefully easier than what Shannon and I have had to learn on our own. As we spend time training our children, they each get progressively easier to train as they get older, but more on this later. Suffice it to say that when you have properly trained your children, you will enjoy spending time with them. And when you spend time with your children, you will have plenty of opportunity to train your children. These two go hand in hand, and pretty soon spending time with your children will be a joy.

One wonderful thing about my children is that they are so forgiving. I know I've made plenty of mistakes with them. I've lost my temper and I've misunderstood what they wanted. I've disciplined the wrong child for things or scolded them when they didn't actually do anything wrong. Yet my children forgive me and still love me. Regardless of what the rest of the world thinks of me, my children love me with their whole heart. It's wonderful to come home after a difficult day at work and know that my kids will be waiting to run to me and tell me about their day and be so glad to see me.

Children have such a unique outlook on the world that sometimes we adults miss. For us, either we've seen it so many times we don't share the wonder anymore, or we see the down side to things instead of the beauty. They don't ignore the simple or the beautiful. My children rejoice when it snows; they don't moan about having to bundle up from the cold or how hard it will be to drive in the snow. They only see the beauty and wonder of snow falling. My children love to bring me endless dandelions from the backyard. I like to let them bring them to me, not only because it brings them such joy to show their love, but also because I don't mind them keeping the dandelion population under control. My children love to look up at the stars in the clear summer night sky, listening intently as we tell them about the stars and constellations. These are all things that are especially good for us adults. Sometimes we get so wrapped up in the daily grind of life that we forget the purpose behind our work and labor. Your children can remind you of the beauty of a weed like a dandelion, of the innocent joy of making mud pies or running in the sprinkler, and the peacefulness of looking up at the night sky.

Children also have a unique way of bringing laughter to people. One or another of my children will do something new and silly, giving us all a round of laughter, especially when the other children join in to copy their sibling. We have many happy times just laughing with them while they are being silly. I was reading the other day that laughter is good for your health, and can even extend your lifespan. Proverbs 15:13 says, "A merry heart makes a cheerful countenance, But by sorrow of the heart the spirit is broken." If this is true, then I'll live a good long time, just because my children are always giving me a good laugh.

Another wonderful thing about raising children is that you are able to teach them about the world and about Christ. This is partly where that maturity in Christ comes from; as you teach your children about Him and they ask you questions, you learn more about Him than you would have done on your own. This is one of the reasons to make sure your relationship with God is solid, because children are excellent at spotting a phony. Teaching your children about the world is wonderful too. None of us can learn everything in school. Somehow no child sees the value in learning all of these things while they have the opportunity. But, as you teach your children, you can, in essence, go back to school with them and learn things you never learned before and refresh your memory about things you have forgotten.

And, of course, there are some more tangible blessings to having many children. As the children get older, they are more able to do chores around the house. As older teenagers they can work and earn considerable income, as well as help around the house. And the tax deduction per child is no small benefit. As our income has grown we have had more children also, but our taxes have stayed the same or gone down, solely because of the extra deductions. Of course none of these should be reasons to have more children, but they are benefits nonetheless.

One benefit that most young, newly married couples don't think about is the blessing of grandchildren one day. My parents say that the best part of having grandchildren is that you get all the joy of the children without most of the work. They have earned the right, by raising me, to spoil my children and leave the training to me. I look forward to doing the same thing for my grandchildren one day, knowing that my children have been trained well and that they will know how to train my grandchildren. This is the godly heritage that the Lord is looking for from His people. And the best part is that it multiplies! The two of us have many children, then they will have many children, then my grandchildren will have many children, and that means there are many godly people inhabiting the earth simply because the two of us were faithful to the Lord and faithful to raise up that godly seed. When we are older we look forward to having to rent a large sports stadium just for family reunions!

And, finally, when I am old and gray, I know I won't lack family to come visit me and even care for me, should I need that. I feel so sorry for the elderly who have nobody to love them or visit them. It's so sad! I look forward to having an endless stream of grandchildren, bringing their own small children, coming to visit me in my old age. And when you have dedicated your life to growing those relationships with your children and grandchildren, they will look forward to visiting you, even when you are old.

CHAPTER 4

Birth "Control"

Who Are We Being "Controlled" By – The World's System or the Lord?

"The Woman Rebel: No Gods, No Masters"– Title of magazine founded in 1914 by Margaret Sanger, birth control activist and Planned Parenthood founder

The following information is not meant to scare or condemn you, and yes, we are not licensed physicians so we challenge you to review the information and our sources and draw your own conclusions. What we do want is for you to be fully informed and make your own decisions based on accurate information, being in agreement as husband and wife. The most important thing is that no matter what decisions you come to, you are responsible for having a clear conscience before the Lord.

History of Birth Control

All through history people have sought to control their fertility. This shouldn't surprise the Christian. God's first instructions to Adam and Eve, before the fall, were that they should "be fruitful and multiply; fill the earth and subdue it; have dominion ... over every living thing that moves on the earth" (Genesis 1:28). Clearly, God desires children, especially from His people. It is the primary vehicle for having dominion over the earth. Because of this, Satan isn't very fond of the idea of humanity multiplying, especially those who obey God. Satan's pattern is to attack everything God creates for good, and fertility is no different. Hence, struggles over birth control have raged for millennia.

Yet we have already seen that the Bible is clear about fertility being a blessing. Early Christians affirmed this view of fertility. Consider the following quotations.

> Clement of Alexandria (?-215 A.D.), *The Instructor, Paedagogus:* "We must regard the woman's crown to be her husband, and the husband's crown to be marriage; and the flowers of marriage the children of both, which the divine husbandman plucks from meadows of flesh. Children's children are the crown of old men."[1]

John Chrysostom, Archbishop of Constantinople, 347-407 A.D., *Homily on Romans 24:* "Why do you sow where the field is eager to destroy the fruit? Where there are medicines of sterility? Where there is murder before birth? You do not even let a harlot remain a harlot, but you make her a murderess as well. Do you see that from drunkenness comes fornication, from fornication adultery, from adultery murder? Indeed, it is something worse than murder and I do not know what to call it; for she does not kill what is formed but prevents its formation. What then? Do you condemn the gift of God, and fight with His laws? What is a curse, do you seek as though it were a blessing?" [2]

Later Christian leaders also agreed that fertility was a blessing from God.

Conrad Dannhauer, 1603-1666: "Although, I say, this sin [destruction of seed] is considered insignificant, indeed, a speck of dust, in the eyes of the world and of the whole of Babylon, it is still in the holy and chaste eyes of God an exceedingly abhorrent and shameful atrocity, more offensive than common whoredom and adultery; because it is more monstrous and runs contrary to nature and God's order. This sin is really an advance murder of that which could have been born of it. Indeed, such filthy persons thereby offer a Molech-sacrifice to the god of the whorish spirit, as the heathen in previous times sacrificed their seed to the idol Molech."[3]

Martin Luther, *Luther's Works, Volume Three:* "...saintly women have always regarded childbirth as a great sign of grace. Rachel is rude and exceedingly irksome to her husband when she says (Gen. 30:1): 'Give me children, or I shall die!' She makes it clear that she will die of grief because she sees barrenness is a sign of wrath. And in Psalm 127:3 there is a glorious eulogy of offspring: 'Lo, sons are a heritage from the Lord, the fruit of the womb is a reward (that is, a gift of God).' Surely it is a magnificent name that children are the gift of God! Therefore Hannah laments so pitiably (1 Sam. 1:10), and John's aged mother Elizabeth leaps for joy and exults (Luke 1:25), 'The Lord has taken away my reproach.' Thus when the world was still in a better state, barrenness was considered a sign of wrath; but childbirth was considered a sign of grace. Because of the abuses of lust, however, this remnant of divine blessing gradually began to be obscured even among the Jews, just as today you could find many greedy men who regard numerous offspring as a punishment. Saintly mothers, however, have always regarded this gift—when they were prolific—as a great honor, just as, conversely, they have regarded barrenness as a sign of wrath and as a reproach."[4]

Teunis Oldenburger, 1934, *Birth Control for Saints and Sinners*: "There is no other exegesis of Scripture possible but to place contraception in the same category with prostitution, free love, homosexuality, coitus interruptus ... and all other forms of unnatural coition that are indulged in simply for the purpose of play, against which both the laws of the land and those of the church have with varying severity been enforced..."[5]

In fact, no denomination gave approval for use of birth control until 1930 when the Anglican Church passed Resolution 15 at the Lambeth Conference, giving limited approval to using birth control. Over the next three decades, the battle raged within the church. Gradually, many other denominations gave their approval to the use of birth control by married couples. By 1961, the National Council of Churches proclaimed that "[m]ost of the Protestant churches hold contraception and periodic abstinence to be morally right when the motives are right." (Feb. 23, 1961) This change in the views within the church reflected the change that was taking place in the views of society at large. The church allowed society to infect it, instead of the church affecting the society.

Margaret Sanger and her National Birth Control League (NBCL) did much of the work done to change societal views toward birth control. In the

United States, the Comstock laws had been passed in the 1870s outlawing contraceptive devices and literature. After her nursing work helping poor mothers deliver their babies, Margaret Sanger decided that birth control would save many of these poor women from their difficult lives. One of the first actions she took to combat the existing laws was to establish the magazine *The Woman Rebel* in 1914. Her claims that the availability of birth control would eliminate the illegal and dangerous abortions women were undergoing influenced many people to aid her cause. Mrs. Sanger was instrumental in changing American attitudes toward birth control, even to the point of coining the term itself and underwriting the research for development of the first human birth control pill in the 1950s. Planned Parenthood, the organization with which most of us are familiar, grew out of the NBCL. It is now the biggest provider of birth control and abortions in America.

On May 9, 1960, the FDA gave approval to the first oral contraceptive. In 1965, the Supreme Court overturned Connecticut's Comstock Laws. These two events opened the door for clinics to dispense birth control information, devices, and oral contraceptives. In response, the Catholic Church addressed the issue of birth control. Pope Paul VI issued *Human Vitae* in 1968, which reaffirmed the Church's historical teaching that "each and every marriage act must remain open to the transmission of life." Subsequent writings by the Catholic Church have upheld this view, and the only form of birth control that they approve is Natural Family Planning, which we will discuss later.

Since the opening of the floodgates, so to speak, that happened in the 1960s, the sexual revolution has continued. In 1973, with the Supreme Court's *Roe vs. Wade* decision, abortion became legal, moving the battle between the church and society from the issue of birth control and contraception to the issue of abortion. Yet the contraception issue hasn't gone away.

Common Birth Control Methods in Use in America Today

In America and much of the Western world, several methods of birth control are widely used. These include hormonal contraception (the Pill, Norplant, Depo-Provera, the patch), barrier methods (condoms, diaphragms), intra-uterine devices (IUDs), spermicidal methods (the sponge, gel, foams, etc), sterilization (tubal ligation, vasectomy), and fertility awareness methods (Natural Family Planning and the Rhythm method). Let's look at each of these to see how they work and what the effects are on the couple using them.

Hormonal Contraception

Hormonal contraception is the most widely used form of birth control in America. It's not hard to see why. It is very effective in preventing life from coming forth, is fairly easy to use, and is most frequently covered by health insurance. The birth control pill (the "Pill") and the birth control patch are generally a combination of estrogen and progesterone. Other forms of hormonal contraception like Norplant and Depo-Provera are progesterone only.

Generally, these methods use several approaches to prevent life. The estrogen is designed to prevent ovulation. If there is no egg, there can be no pregnancy, so preventing ovulation is very effective contraception. The problem is that excess estrogen in a woman's system causes a multitude of other problems. When the Pill was first licensed for use in the U.S., women complained of many unpleasant side effects. Manufacturers of the Pill responded by reducing the dose of estrogen in the pills. Currently, the levels are a fairly low dose, considered by many to be a "safe level" even when used constantly for many consecutive years. Recently, researchers have discovered that the patch gives a higher dose of hormones than the pill because of the different delivery method. Many users of the patch are experiencing the same side effects that were common with early versions of the pill.

If this was the only consequence of these products, it might not be so bad, but the story of what the progesterone does is not so innocent. The effect of the progesterone, in the progesterone-only formulations like Norplant and Depo-Provera, is to cause the endometrial lining to be thinner. That sounds ok, but the effect of this is that a fertilized egg (if you ovulated in spite of the estrogen in your pills) would be unable to implant in the uterus. Doctors who work in the field of In-Vitro Fertilization ("test tube" babies) have discovered that if the endometrial lining is less than 8.5mm in thickness, the embryos have a significantly decreased chance of implantation and growth. The ideal (and normal) thickness during the expected time of implantation during a woman's cycle is 11mm. Some studies of the effect of hormonal birth control on the endometrial thickness have measured it as low as 6mm. Obviously, progesterone use in hormonal contraception is designed to prevent implantation of a fertilized egg. That means they are abortifacient – it causes a spontaneous abortion (also called a miscarriage; in this case a very early miscarriage) of the baby.

Now, I know many of you who are now taking the Pill or using the patch, or who have in the past, are saying that nobody told you that this would make you miscarry any child you might conceive. I agree – nobody told me (Shannon) either, and I was on the Pill for nine years. Even worse is the information that the current low-dose estrogen pills allow for more "escape-ovulation," which means that you produce a fertile egg despite the effects of the Pill. According to Dr. Chris Kahlenborn, "One can conclude that escape-ovulation is a natural event straining to occur if a tablet is missed, or not properly absorbed due to illness or drug interaction."[6] The incidence of escape-ovulation with Norplant is known to be higher, and Depo-Provera works the same way, so it is logical to believe that it also acts as an abortifacient. Imagine my sorrow and distress to discover that I might have conceived and miscarried as many as *one child every year while I was on the pill!*[7] That revelation just about broke my heart, and it is part of the reason for writing this book. Many people in the world don't see the significance of this, but Christians, especially "pro-life" Christians, should be shaken to their core by this information. In case you are still wondering if this is true, see the Resources at the end of this book for sources that provide further evidence that forms of hormonal birth control are abortifacients, and that the drug companies and Planned Parenthood have known it and admitted it all along.

If you are still interested in using hormonal birth control, here is some more information about other side effects experienced by many women, especially when taken for several years, as most women do. Dr. Kahlenborn states that, "Both of these forms of hormonal contraception [oral contraceptives and Depo-Provera] radically increase the risk of breast cancer when given to young women, especially if they are used before the age of first childbirth."[8] He reports a 40% increased risk of breast cancer if a woman uses the Pill before delivering her first child, and a 72% increased risk if she used the pill for more than four years prior to her first child. He also reports that women who used Depo-Provera for two to three years before the age of 25 have a 190% increased risk for breast cancer. These are sobering numbers to say the least, but they are just the beginning of the effects of hormonal contraception on a woman's body. Liver tumors have been found in higher numbers in younger women (ages 15 to 40), which corresponds with the increased use of oral contraceptives in this age group.[9] Women using the Pill have a 3 to 11 times increased risk of developing blood clots that can lead to stroke and heart attack. Risk of fatal heart attacks is approximately two times higher in women taking the Pill, and the risk of fatal brain hemorrhage is 1.4 times higher. Among women who smoke and take the Pill, these risks are even higher.[10]

Studies as early as 1975 showed that users of hormonal contraception showed deficiencies in folate and vitamin B12. Research since that time has showed that these women are also deficient in thiamine, riboflavin, niacin and pyridoxine (all of these are B vitamins). Other deficiencies found in users of the Pill are vitamin C, magnesium, selenium, zinc, and copper. Women taking the Pill commonly have increased levels of triglycerides and an imbalance of HDL to LDL cholesterol. Eighty-five to ninety percent of mothers with children diagnosed with ADD or ADHD had been on hormonal contraception at some point prior to conceiving the child.[11] These nutritional deficiencies lead to a myriad of physical ailments including muscle weakness, fatigue, irritability, depression, poor digestion, premature wrinkles, headaches, nausea, anxiety, graying hair, low infection resistance, thyroid insufficiency, prolonged wound healing, hyperglycemia (a precursor to diabetes), premature birth, low birth weight, and preeclampsia. In November 2004, the FDA has added a "black box" warning on Depo-Provera warning that prolonged use of this drug can lead to bone density loss, and that the loss is greater the longer the drug is used. This bone density loss may not be completely reversible after discontinuation of the drug, and the FDA is recommending that women only use this form of contraception if other alternatives prove inadequate.[12] Most recently, researchers have found that many women experience a long term (perhaps permanent) loss of libido after taking the Pill, even after they are no longer taking it. [13] Lloyd J. DuPlantis, Jr, P.D., makes a very astute observation:

"Today, the media and many in mainstream American medicine indicate that it is politically correct for young women to focus on diet, exercise and nutritional supplementation for overall health and well-being. Paradoxically, these same sources encourage the taking of steroidal hormones, which have been shown to have all these negative health consequences, almost as soon as a young girl reaches puberty. Following this wisdom, they would then have her remain on this regimen until old age, stopping only for those few brief moments when popular consensus has it that the appropriate time has arrived to conceive..."[14]

Barrier and Spermicide

Many couples that do not want to use hormonal contraception use a barrier or spermicidal method. Most barrier methods include spermicide to increase effectiveness, so we will discuss them together. Disadvantages of using barrier and spermicidal methods include messiness, interruption of foreplay, decreased pleasure (especially with the condom), and the lesser effectiveness at avoiding the bringing forth of life.

More serious risks of these methods of contraception include increased risk of miscarriage[15] and birth defects[16] if a pregnancy does result. Also, some spouses have an allergic reaction to the latex used in condoms and to the chemicals used in spermicidal foams and jellies. The sponge can cause toxic shock syndrome. Diaphragms can increase the risk of bladder infections. Barrier methods have also been linked to increased risk of preeclampsia, a serious complication of pregnancy. "Women who rely on birth control methods, such as condoms and diaphragms, that prevent semen from reaching the uterus, are more than twice as likely to develop [preeclampsia] as are their counterparts who had been repeatedly exposed to sperm from the prospective father."[17]

Perhaps the most serious risk to those who would use a spermicide called nonoxynol-9, either alone or in conjunction with a barrier method, is the increased risk of acquiring the AIDS virus and other sexually transmitted diseases.

The Food and Drug Administration (FDA) has proposed new warning labels for over-the-counter vaginal contraceptive drugs that contain spermicide nonoxynol-9 (N-9). The new label would state that vaginal contraceptives containing N-9 do not protect against infection from HIV or other sexually transmitted diseases (STDs). The proposed warnings would say that vaginal contraceptives containing N-9 increase vaginal [and anal] irritation, which may heighten the possibility of acquiring the AIDS virus and other STDs.[18]

Intra-Uterine Device (IUD)

Intra-uterine devices (IUDs) have been used as another form of contraceptive. They are touted as easier to use than barrier methods and as effective as hormonal methods without having to remember to take a pill every day.

There are two types of IUDs. One kind emits a chemical that is intended to have an anti-sperm effect. The other kind only works mechanically. Generally, both types of IUD prevent implantation of a fertilized egg, so therefore both are abortifacients. Even if the chemicals emitted by some IUDs have an anti-sperm effect, it is clear that the IUDs are at least some of the time, if not most of the time, abortifacients.

The IUD carries many risks for the woman as well. The device can cause permanent damage to the uterus, making future pregnancies virtually impossible. It can cause severe abdominal pain from perforation or infection of the uterus, and increase bleeding during menstruation. It causes Pelvic Inflammatory Disease (PID), and the FDA requires each device to carry a warning to that effect. If a pregnancy does result, it is more likely to be ectopic.[19]

Sterilization

Sterilization is increasingly becoming the contra-ception method of choice, even among Christians. Many couples decide that they have enough children. Some decide that they are too old to have more children. Some decide that they have health issues regarding pregnancy or raising their children. Regardless of the reason, sterilization has become accepted and commonplace.

Yet these procedures also have risks of their own. Female sterilization (tubal ligation, commonly known as "having your tubes tied") can cause bladder infections, painful intercourse, pelvic pain or pressure, and increased cervical cancer rate. It can make PMS worse. It can also complicate menstruation by worsening cramps and causing abnormal bleeding (longer and heavier bleeding as well as mid-cycle bleeding). Frequently the blood supply to the ovaries is compromised, resulting in hormone shifts that can mimic premenopause. The surgery itself carries the risks of general anesthesia (if used), injury to the bowel, bladder and blood vessels, and infection.

Male sterilization, or vasectomy, also carries long-term risks. Among the most serious are the autoimmune diseases that can result. This is because the body continues to produce sperm at the normal rate, but they are not expelled in the previous way. When the body breaks them down to remove them, it causes an autoimmune reaction. This reaction can be measured as early as two weeks after the procedure. Studies show that many diseases are considered to be related to autoimmunity, including multiple sclerosis, diabetes, rheumatoid arthritis, and lupus. One study determined that "the immunologic response to sperm antigen that often accompanies vasectomy can exacerbate atherosclerosis" (hardening of the arteries).[20]

Another possible risk of vasectomy is increased risk of prostate cancer. One study found the risk to increase by 3.5-5.3 times.[21] Another found an overall risk of 1.7 times greater beginning twelve years after the procedure, rising to 2.2 times the risk thirteen to eighteen years later.[22] Studies from Harvard Medical School found that the overall risk increased 56-60%, increasing to 89% for those who had vasectomies 20 or more years earlier.[23] Other risks include kidney stones, testicular cancer, testicular atrophy, change in testosterone production, and Post-Vasectomy Pain Syndrome (PVP). This last one, PVP, is particularly devastating. Here is a portion of a post on the discussion forum of www.dontfixit.org with a bit of personal testimony:

> In Oct. 99 I had a closed-ended vasectomy. I started developing pain three days after... I finally got completely well after eleven months. I was pain free for six months until one day I was jumping and playing basketball, followed by a leg hamstring work out. A couple of hours later the pain sensation returned. The only diagnosis I have received is scar tissue nerve entrapment. My condition has improved some but with any minor activity the pressure, swelling, and pain

sensation returns. My treatment approach has been very conservative; [I'm] hoping that time will help me heal. Other non-invasive treatment consists of medications, physical therapy, swimming etc. Nothing has worked. Sometimes my pain is severe and I miss work. Other times I just grind it out... PVP has changed my life. I have two kids that I can't play with; I can't do any housework or yard work. I can no longer work out [in the gym] or golf. I cannot walk or sit for an extended time. Everything I do revolves around PVP. This has not only affected me, but my family as well. I would like to explore some treatment options, but I have not heard of any treatment options that work. It sounds like everything causes more discomfort.[24]

While some couples ultimately choose to reverse their sterilization, many find that they are unable to conceive or that the reversal doesn't resolve the health issues caused by the original sterilization procedure. They also find that while their health insurance probably paid for the original procedure, they must fund the reversal on their own.

Natural Family Planning

Natural Family Planning (NFP) is when the couple tracks the phases of the woman's fertility cycle and abstains from marital relations during the period when she is most fertile. This method used to be referred to as the Rhythm Method, although it has gotten much more sophisticated in recent years, increasing the effectiveness. This is the only method of birth control approved by the Catholic Church.

Of all the forms of birth control, NFP is the least offensive. As Christians, however, we are not to be guided by what is least offensive. We are to be guided by what is scriptural. Therefore, we need to examine NFP in light of Scripture.

The general premise of NFP is that the couple using it for birth control should abstain for a period of time during the woman's fertile part of her cycle. For those couples that are using this method to regulate your family size, we are grateful that you have taken the time to research contraceptive methods. We do not equate this method with abortion or the abortifacient nature of other methods, and this method is not physically harmful to the couple using it, as many other contraceptives are.

We would, however, encourage you to take an honest look at your motivations for using this method. Consider Romans 12:1: "I beseech you therefore, brethren, by the mercies of God, that you present your bodies a living sacrifice, holy, acceptable to God, *which is* your reasonable service." Our bodies and our lives are to be a sacrifice to the Lord. This is only "reasonable" of Him to ask of us. We need to sacrifice our own desires, thoughts, and goals, and instead take up His desires, His thoughts, and His goals. As a couple we need to stand before the Lord with a clear conscience.

When you study the Old Testament Laws regarding abstinence during a woman's cycle as outlined in Leviticus 15 in light of what we now know about a woman's fertility cycle, you realize that one of the side effects of this law is increased fertility, not avoidance of conception. A woman was considered unclean for seven days, or until the end of her bleeding. During this time, if a man came in contact with her blood, he would also be unclean for seven days. This made it very unlikely that they would have any relations during this time. So, when a married couple would come together again after her seven days of being unclean, she would be very close to her time of being fertile. Also, the husband would have a higher concentration of sperm because of his week of abstinence. These two factors combined to increase the likelihood of conception.

We have already discussed how God views children as a blessing and a reward, and how He has given procreation to humanity as an instruction (Gen. 1:28). Also consider Isaiah 55: 8-9: "For My thoughts *are* not your thoughts, nor *are* your ways My ways," says the LORD. For *as* the heavens are higher than the earth, so are My ways higher than your ways, and My thoughts than your thoughts." How can we presume to make this decision apart from the Lord, based on our own thoughts and our own wisdom? His ways are higher than ours. His thoughts are higher than ours. He can see the end from the beginning. How can our own wisdom possibly compare? We must seek His guidance on this issue, together as a couple, and not just make a decision based on our own wisdom and desires. We'll talk more about coming to agreement as a couple in a later chapter.

Abortion

Some of you might wonder why we include abortion in a discussion of birth control methods. The reason is because throughout the ages, as people have sought to control their fertility, their methods have included true contraception (prevention of conception) as well as abortion and even infanticide, should the attempts at preventing or interrupting the pregnancy fail. And, as we have seen, many of our modern methods of birth control actually cause abortions, at least some of the time. Birth control and abortion are two sides of the same coin in that they alter a process that could potentially result in a new life. They are both non-reproductive as their basis. I believe that God loves children and would want to bless us with them.

In researching the history of birth control, it struck me how the progression was made from having the churches begin to accept birth control to having the society at large accept it to having abortion legalized. I was also struck by the way Margaret Sanger used the same reasons for birth control that are used to justify abortion today. She claimed that the widespread use of birth control would save women from the dangerous "back alley" abortions. Apparently it didn't, because fifty years later, in spite of widespread acceptance and use of birth control, we heard the same thing about so-called "safe, legal" abortions. As

I said at the beginning of this chapter, once abortion became legal, the battle against birth control changed into the battle against abortion. Yet those outside the church see that we readily accept birth control even while we condemn abortion. I believe this dichotomy leaves the unchurched confused. They know that birth control and abortion are both anti-procreation, thus they are variations on the same theme. In their mind, they both have the same outcome. To many of them, the ends justify the means.

> *"Disturbing, too, is the realization that both birth control and abortion have exactly the same effect (through substantially different means), namely, the prevention of another human being. The one kills the product of conception, the other prevents conception; but both aim to prevent the birth of a person. The failure to prevent conception has led many to murder the mistake that results. Isn't it reasonable to conclude that commonly behind both acts there is the same love of self and hatred of God? Has not the birth control mindset been the mother of the abortion mindset? Certainly the two are connected in our culture. Whether it is possible to separate the two is another question, but the connection should give Christians pause."*[25]

> *"There is an unarguable logic connecting the contraceptive act and the abortive act. They are both anti-life. To fully articulate this*

51

proposition, the contraceptive action is anti-the-formation of a new life. One does not pop a pill, slip on a condom and take a shot in the buttocks, etc. in preparation for a game of Chinese checkers. The only logical reason for these actions is to prevent the formation of a new life while positing voluntary coital acts."[26]

[W]e have a tremendous demand from [adoptive] couples who cannot have a child - but I never give a child to a couple who [has] done something not to have a child [used contraception].... In destroying the power of giving life, through contraception, a husband or wife is doing something to self. This turns the attention to self and so it destroys the gifts of love in him or her.... Once that living love is destroyed by contraception, abortion follows very easily.... We cannot solve all the problems in the world, but let us never bring in the worst problem of all, and that is to destroy love. And this is what happens when we tell people to practice contraception and abortion."[27] *(Mother Theresa)*

I believe this is why the church has not been more successful in the pro-life movement. We are presenting the unchurched with a paradox. We say we are pro-life, yet we limit our own fertility. We try to fight against abortion, yet we have not fully embraced God's vision for our own procreation. We have tried to ride on the fence in the matter. We reject abortion because it is such an assault on our senses, but we still want to control our own lives and our own bodies. This is very much what the pro-choice movement is all about – being able to control their own lives and their own bodies, only for them that includes after conception. I believe this is one war we cannot win until we get off the fence and totally come over to God's side, accepting His design for our lives. In the next chapter, we will explore what would happen if every Christian would become Quiver^X, and we will look at some of the consequences of the widespread application of birth control within the church.

CHAPTER 5

Confront Our Enemies in the Gates
Take Back What the Enemy Stole From Us

Then God blessed them, and God said to them, "Be fruitful and multiply; fill the earth and subdue it; have dominion over the fish of the sea, over the birds of the air, and over every living thing that moves on the earth." Genesis 1:28

God is all about multiplication, not just addition.

Exodus 1:7-10 — "But the children of Israel were fruitful and increased abundantly, multiplied and grew exceedingly mighty; and the land was filled with them. Now there arose a new king over Egypt, who did not know Joseph. And he said to his people, 'Look, the people of the children of Israel are more and mightier than we; come, let us deal shrewdly with them, lest they multiply, and it happen, in the event of war, that they also join our enemies and fight against us, and so go up out of the land.'"

If we allow the Lord to bless us with as many children as He chooses, and we teach those children diligently and they teach their children diligently, then we will be able to overwhelm the enemy by sheer numbers. Consider Figure 5.1:

Figure 5.1

Families each having 5 children	Families each having 2 children

 YOUR CHILDREN

5 CHILDREN
7 PEOPLE TOTAL

2 CHILDREN
4 PEOPLE TOTAL

 YOUR GRAND CHILDREN

25 CHILDREN
32 PEOPLE TOTAL

4 CHILDREN
8 PEOPLE TOTAL

 YOUR GREAT GRAND CHILDREN

125 CHILDREN
157 PEOPLE TOTAL

8 CHILDREN
16 PEOPLE TOTAL

 YOUR GREAT, GREAT GRAND CHILDREN

625 CHILDREN
782 PEOPLE TOTAL

16 CHILDREN
32 PEOPLE TOTAL

You can see from this illustration that the multi-plication effect of having many children is dramatic! Keep in mind that this chart depicts direct lineage only, assuming five children born to each family in each generation, and does not include spouses of the descendants.

Now, consider if the "YOU" represented the church in the United States in the year 1930 when the church first began to accept birth control, in Figure 5.2 below:

Figure 5.2

| <u>Families each
having 5 children</u> | <u>Families each
having 2 children</u> |

 YOUR CHILDREN 1930

5 CHILDREN
7 PEOPLE TOTAL

2 CHILDREN
4 PEOPLE TOTAL

 YOUR GRAND CHILDREN 1950

25 CHILDREN
32 PEOPLE TOTAL

4 CHILDREN
8 PEOPLE TOTAL

 YOUR GREAT GRAND CHILDREN 1970

125 CHILDREN
157 PEOPLE TOTAL

8 CHILDREN
16 PEOPLE TOTAL

 **YOUR GREAT, GREAT GRAND CHILDREN 1990**

625 CHILDREN
782 PEOPLE TOTAL

16 CHILDREN
32 PEOPLE TOTAL

Imagine where our society would be today had we followed the left side, the Lord's plan for families, rather than embracing the world's ways, as depicted on the right side. Imagine the political, social, financial, and other ramifications that would have been the result of a church that had not selfishly embraced the things of the world (i.e., birth control), but rather chose to walk victoriously in what God had planned for our country. Looking at the illustration, is it any wonder why the Church has seemingly been losing the culture war in our society?

With all of the "alternative" lifestyles out there today, it would only take a generation of Quiver^x Christians and we would just plain outnumber the forces of the enemy; in many respects we do outnumber them now, but we are not really in the battle. A lot of our troops are spectators and not participants. It is much easier to watch the game than it is to play in the game. As it says in Psalm 127:5 (NIV): "Blessed is the man whose Quiver is full of them. They will not be put to shame when they contend with their enemies in the gate." When I contend with my enemies in the gate, I want as many God-provided arrows with me as He sees fit to bless me with. Whether they contend with the enemies in the gate by bringing a scientific cure for cancer, or whether they are a great prophet or evangelist, or whether they are a greeter every Sunday at the local church, may the Lord give each of them five talents and may they all double those talents in service to the Lord. I may use a lot of language that seems like I am really expecting a lot from my children.

Why not? Each of them, with God helping them, can accomplish anything He has planned for them. Eddie Windsor, author of *Increasing Your Personal Capacity*, said, "If you are going to raise children, why not raise champions?"

These demonstrations have used the assumption of five children in each family. This is a conservative estimate since many families could have had more than five. Consider what would have happened if this number had been multiplied by a thousand Christian families across the country, or by a million families. Where would the church be today? What would our society look like? Imagine the influence we would have had on our culture over the years if this had been the case.

Now is the time for the church to turn back to the Lord's ways. We need to return to God's plan for His people, by welcoming children into our families in His name. It's not too late to impact our society for Christ in this manner. If we start now, with this current generation, we can see those bigger numbers of Christians in the generations of our grandchildren and our great grandchildren. In the 21st century we could completely change the landscape of our society – politically, socially, economically, and religiously. What a legacy to leave!

The time for making this change in our thinking couldn't be more crucial. Consider the following quote, from the Boston Globe, February 22, 2004, regarding the growing number of healthy, successful adults who are choosing to remain childless:

Over the last decade, the movement's been growing. Today, there are numerous support groups such as No Kidding, which was launched in 1984 and has a fast-growing number of chapters in big cities in the United States and around the world. The Internet now has countless e-mail groups and Web pages — www.childfree.net, www.overpopulation. org, to name two — dedicated to people who don't have kids....

Larson, the newspaper reporter, is 42 and handsome, with wavy hair and a neatly trimmed beard. "It's easy to be won over by the bundle of joy that comes out of the mother's womb, and 'Oh, how cute' and 'Oh, how nice,' but then not be prepared for the actual sacrifices that are going to have to be made, ...I know if I had kids, I would not be able to do the things I enjoy now. I would have to give up going to events with friends. I would have to give up part of my writing projects. I wouldn't be able to go out to concerts as much as I like, or go to museums, or take courses."...

It's an increasingly popular sentiment and part of a growing tension, particularly as the number of child-free adults grows. A report released last year by the Rutgers University National Marriage Project shows that fewer people — just one-third of American households — are choosing to have children. That's down from 80 percent in the mid-1800s and 50 percent in 1960. By 2010, the U.S. Census Bureau projects, just one-quarter of all American households will have children living in them....

All this is profoundly troubling to Rutgers professor David Popenoe, who coauthored the study and co-directs the marriage project. He thinks the child-free are hitting enough of a critical mass to mobilize a culture war that pits them against people in more traditional families: mother, father, kids. "In public life in America, the shift has been away from child-centeredness," he says. "You already see this in zoning and the cases of building housing deliberately to discourage children and their effects on tax dollars. You have schools under attack more than ever before, turning down bond issues, and the feeling that if you have children, you should therefore pay for them and don't expect us to pay for them. I just think it would be a national tragedy if the culture war were extended to the issue of children versus no children," Popenoe says. "But it could well be a big issue in the future as you have more and more people who are single and childless."[1]

If the church doesn't make a change in their thinking — and more importantly, in their actions

– now, it will be harder to make that change in the future when there is even more societal pressure against having children at all, let alone being willing to have a large family. But, the good news is that if society at large is decreasing the number of children they have, that will increase our own impact if we begin to have larger families. The time to procreate is now!

CHAPTER 6

We Can't Afford It
Stretch Your Faith as You Stretch Your Family Size

"[Some] complain of the scantiness of their means, and allege that they have not enough for bringing up more children, as though, in truth, their means were in [their] power . . . or God did not daily make the rich poor and the poor rich." (Lactantius, Divine Institutes 6:20 [A.D. 307]).

First of all, we must remember that our children are first God's children. He is the one who knew them before the foundation of the world. He is the one who gave them to us. He is the one who laid His life down on the cross for them. He is the one who has a great and wonderful plan for their lives. We need to recognize that the Lord loves our children even more than we do, and we need to recognize from the Scriptures that they are a reward from God.

> Psalm 127:3 — "Behold, children are a heritage from the Lord, The fruit of the womb is a reward."

We have established that the fruit of the womb (children) is God's reward. That's Bible. I didn't make it up myself; God wrote it a long time ago. Think about this. What if some rich philanthropist came up to you one day and said, "You know what, I like your lifestyle. I am going to deposit $1000 per week into your bank account for the rest of your life." How many of you would accept the rich man's rewards for a few months or years and then call the wealthy benefactor and tell him, "You know, I've had enough. I can't take being a good steward of your generous resources anymore. I am having difficulty with managing all the money properly. Would you kindly stop placing money into my bank account?"

I don't think any of us would say, "No more money, please." We would take classes or hire a financial advisor or otherwise rise to the occasion of handling the money, because we would recognize the value and power of what the wealthy benefactor has entrusted to us. Church, we need to do the same with our children. We have said, "No thanks Lord, I've had enough," or, "I can't take it anymore," or "My children are out of control," or, "I can't afford it anymore," or, "I really want to take a vacation sometime to Australia, and that will never happen if I keep having children," or "Sorry, Lord, but I just don't trust You enough to provide for the reward (child) that you have given to us, to provide for the children that You have a grand plan for, to provide for these children that You died on the cross for. Would you kindly stop rewarding us?" We need to recognize the value and power in what God has entrusted to us. If we are struggling to be good stewards of these blessings, we need to seek God for wisdom or take classes or hire help or otherwise rise to the occasion, not seek to limit the blessing.

Please hear our hearts on this; children are His reward, but faith is not faith if you can do it on your own. God knows that we will find ourselves in places where we can't do it ourselves. That is when the miracle comes! If we are never in a position of need, at the end of our own ability to deal with the situation, we will never be poised to receive a miracle from the Lord. Sometimes the Lord provides consistently, like through a steady job, and sometimes He brings a miracle. Either way, be sure to give Him the glory.

Sometimes, though, our financial difficulties are our own making. The Lord constantly wants to take us to the next level in all areas, including finances. Ongoing or long-term financial problems are usually a result of poor stewardship or poor management. I know that in my own life this has been one of my greatest struggles.

When we had only one child, I (Jim) had no clue how I would "afford" (in my own mind) any more children. I used to think, "I am barely getting by now.

How can I handle another mouth to feed?" I can also tell you that after my wife and I prayed and came to the decision to be Quiver^x and we had our first son, the Lord began to teach me principles of financial management. I also began to increase financially in my vocation working with computers. Every time a new child came along I received another increase in my job. God is faithful!

Let me tell you a little story from my own life. There was a period after I was "dot-com'd" that I was unemployed for about four months. This happened just before our 4th child was born. This was to be one of my greatest trials and one of my greatest victories in the Lord. I thought, "This is it, the family is going to fall apart. We're going to end up on the street, and I will surely die homeless, without my family," for I imagined that they would definitely move on and find someone who could better provide for them. (Oh, just a side note: we should be very careful about our faith levels. A low faith level can lead to pity parties and more serious depression, which do nothing but destroy the very things that the Lord is trying to work in us. When our faith levels are low, we need to hold tight to the Lord and surround ourselves with other people who have higher faith levels until we get back on our feet again.)

My job was my identity and I was very good at what I did. I was very good at earning money to provide for my family. Of course my statement earlier about "faith not being faith if I can do it myself" rang through my mind during my whole season of unemployment. The Lord was teaching me that He alone was my source, not my job or myself. The other big lesson He was teaching me was about stewardship. He wanted me to learn how to properly handle the "talents" and finances that He had given me. I believe that He does normally provide through the husband being employed, but during this season of my life the Lord wanted to clearly demonstrate and teach me that He alone was my source. And do you know what? During those four months, He did provide. Sure, I received unemployment compensation, but it was a little less than half of what I had been earning. One of the things I had done when I went to work for the dot-com was to run out and buy a new mini-van. I was intoxicated by my new raise and how much money I was now making. Mind you, our other mini-van ran and looked fine, but it was older, with a lot more miles and didn't look as cool (this can sometimes be an important aspect for men) as our new mini-van. But the old mini-van was paid for. The new one was (gulp) … financed at … (squirms a little bit more) a high interest rate. (Just another side note — I believe that as Christians we should strive to be debt free. There may be things like a house or a car that we may choose to finance, but our goal and our stewardship mentality needs to be one of working to be completely, 100%, totally debt free.) I thought "Hey, what does it matter, I am making really good money now and had 50,000 shares of stock in my new company. Things are only going up from here, right?" Well, we all know what happened when the grotesquely over-inflated market finally began to vanish like the fog it really was. My dot-com was no different than all the rest of them, and my stock certificates were now suitable only for kindling.

We scaled back a lot during this time and realized that we didn't need a lot of the services, toys, internet, video games, cable TV, etc., that we thought we did. We made it through that time by the grace of God. We didn't have anything repossessed, we never went hungry, and we never got evicted from where we lived. We were successful at scaling back, and we were able to pay everything we owed everybody every month (including our tithe to our local church). God is good! He is never late, but He will sometimes come through at what we perceive to be the very last minute just to stretch our faith a bit more.

That's enough about me. Let's talk about having more children. Having more children does not necessarily burn up more of your financial resources. Let's say for instance that it takes $5000 per year to support your first child. Each child after that is NOT another $5000 per year. The cost of having and raising subsequent children is much, much lower because resources are shared and passed down. You already have a vehicle to transport the child, and you can probably transport two children in the same vehicle for the same cost. (Yes, you will need to upgrade to a larger vehicle as you have more children, but you can still purchase vehicles that fit your budget.) You already have a home or apartment, and you can probably have two children in that bedroom as easily as you can have one. (Yes, it would be nice to have a bigger house once you have many children, but I know several very large families who live in very modestly-sized houses. You just have to invest in bunk beds and use space wisely.)

There are even more ways to be frugal to stretch your budget as your family grows. There is no rule that says you must go out and buy a whole new wardrobe for each child every year. Maybe our modern advertisers would like you to think that, but it's simply not necessary. My wife saves all the children's clothes (except those worn by our teenage daughter) so they can be passed down to the next child. Of course, she throws away clothes that are worn out or stained, but generally when the child outgrows that size of clothes they are stored in a box for the next child to grow into. Then we don't have to buy very many new clothes for the child when they grow to the next size, just a few things here and there. Most of those are purchased either on sale or from a good second-hand store. (We are blessed in our area to have wonderful second-hand stores.) Garage sales and websites like eBay are also great places to find good deals on clothes, if you have the time and inclination to visit them. When your children are little, save money on their clothes by purchasing them as inexpensively as possible. The time will come when they won't be so happy with second-hand clothes and you'll have to get good at buying clothes on sale. But, teenagers aren't as likely to get spaghetti stains on their clothes, so your clothing dollars will go further once they get to that age.

Another important area where you can conserve money is in your food budget. The most important thing to saving money in your food budget is to be organized. When we only had one child we could afford to stop at the store whenever we needed something, eat frozen TV dinners, eat out regularly, and buy lots of convenience foods. As our food budget has gotten tighter, we started planning the main meals for each week and started keeping a grocery list. We have also moved to making more things from scratch at home. It's much less expensive (and better for you) to cook from scratch rather than buying pre-made foods, but it does take some planning ahead. Make a good list so you don't buy too many impulse items (unless they are something you will use anyway and they are a good price), and strive to buy most of your foods from the outside aisles of the grocery store (dairy, meat, fruits, veggies, etc). We try to buy very little of the pre-boxed, pre-bagged, pre-processed foods in most of the aisles. Buying in bulk is another wonderful money saver in exchange for a bit of storage space. Some families really get their money's worth from warehouse clubs, especially if you get a discounted membership. Also, for items that you use a lot (for us, it's disposable diapers), check out the company's website and see if they will send you coupons, or buy coupons online (see our Resources section for our favorites). We still get coupons for our brand of diapers every month. To inspire you, Shannon was just talking to a mother of seven children who spends only about $125 per week on her groceries, and she lives in a very small town so her prices are higher than many of us pay. No, her children aren't starving! She has learned to really get her money's worth from everything she buys, and to be wise in her purchases. Ironically, when you change your diet to a more healthful one, including lots of whole grains and homemade foods, your grocery costs will go down. Sounds like a good change to me!

Probably the best advice I can give you, though, regarding managing your finances to be good stewards of the Lord's provision, has two parts. First, tithe – every time, cheerfully. Make it a habit so you don't even sweat about writing that check. Make it automatic. Second, get a good budget established and stick to it. We use the Money Matters software from Crown Financial Concepts (Larry Burkett's ministry) and love it. See our Resources section for more information about getting some of their budgeting materials. Generally, though, a good budget is more than just a spending plan. A spending plan is a plan about what you are going to spend your money on and when. That's a good start, but a budget is more than that. A budget makes sure you have the money for regular expenses AND occasional expenses. If you are on a good budget, you should never fall behind in your taxes or your annual insurance premium because you have set aside enough each month to pay them when they are due. You also don't stress about buying Christmas presents because you have been setting aside a little bit of money all year so you have a Christmas fund to use for shopping. Ideally, once your vehicle is paid off you should continue to pay yourself a car payment (into savings) so that when you need to replace or repair your vehicle, you have funds to use. When you do this with all of your budget areas, you'll have the money for that medical bill or vacation or whatever because you've been planning ahead.

Most importantly, remember that your children love **you**, not the things you can provide for them. Nobody, while lying on their deathbed, wishes they had bought a better car or given their child that cool toy for Christmas. They regret that they didn't spend more time with their families, or that the time they spent wasn't happy time. The best gift you can give your children is YOU! Don't get caught up in materialism and coveting what your neighbors or your friends have. Give yourself to your children – your time, your attention, your help, your approval, your love, and your faith – and you will have given them more than the world.

When I think of all my blessings,
the greatest of my joys,
My parents gave me siblings,
instead of rooms of toys.
[Author unknown]

CHAPTER 7

My Choice, My Body
Don't Make a Doctrine, and Real Women Have Stretch Marks

"Few realize that up until 1930, all Protestant denominations agreed with the Catholic Church's teaching condemning contraception as sinful." Catholic Answers, "Birth Control" (San Diego: Catholic Answers, 2001)[1]

This is one of the major issues I hope the reader understands by now. The devil, our flesh, and the world system have all lied to the church for far too long. Please understand, it is not our intention to sit in the seat of judgment. We do NOT want to TELL you what to do. We believe each person will someday stand before the Lord to give an account for their actions, and the most important thing is for each of us to continually have a clear conscience before the Lord on all matters. We want to educate the church about this large area that we are allowing to go untended. We have been neglecting our own vines in order to pursue our own interests.

God has included sexuality in us in the form of each of us requiring intimacy. In addition to wanting intimacy with other people like our spouse or parents or children, He created us to want intimacy with Him. We have tried very hard to replace that intimacy with many things, but only real intimacy with God through a relationship with Jesus Christ can truly bring fulfillment of the longing that we have. When we try to replace that relationship, that intimacy, with other things, it leads us away from the things of God. This is one of the reasons why God did not want Israel getting mixed up with other cultures; He knew that those cultures would tend to be a substitute for His intimate relationship with them, and many times that is exactly what happened.

Malachi 2:15 gives an important explanation of God's goals for marriage.

"But did He not make them one [husband and wife], having a remnant of the Spirit? And why one? He seeks godly offspring. Therefore take heed to your spirit, and let none deal treacherously with the wife of his youth."

In this passage, the Lord makes it clear that one of His purposes for marriage is to raise up godly seed, to procreate and teach those children to serve Him. We need to follow God's entire plan for marriage, including this aspect.

For those of you that like to see things graphed out, here is a formula for you.

Sexuality (or desiring intimacy)
+
Non-procreative mindsets (having fun without the possibility of conception)
=
Road to perversion (adultery, homosexuality, masochism, alternate lifestyles, etc.)

When a husband and wife want to "have fun" without thought of having children, the "having fun" will eventually become not enough. They will try to fulfill their longing by branching out into perversions, trying to get a level of thrill or fulfillment. But that fulfillment can only be found by having godly intimacy, which includes allowing the possibility of having children.

It is important for us to know the truth. Jesus was full of grace and truth. We need to walk in truth, and hopefully you have seen that we are trying to speak the truth in love. The truth is that there are many areas in our society that have been negatively affected by our choices to not follow God's ways because of our own selfishness. We human beings would rather be doing almost anything other than what the Lord really wants us to do. The problems that the church has created extend into many areas of our society simply because we bought into the lies of the enemy. The enemy has tried very hard to make the modern church of little or no effect. He told us to stop having children because "it is too hard." He told us to not get involved in politics, so we stayed out of politics because "things are messy in the political arenas." He told us to keep out of the media, newspapers, TV, and Hollywood. We are seeing and reaping from the seeds that have been sown in our country for decades.

The issue of same-sex marriage is one of these areas that has cropped up specifically because we have not protected marriage. Since birth control became acceptable within the church and in society in general, the institution of marriage has begun to decay. As the purpose of marriage was redefined, from being that of a self-less purpose of building a family for the good of the family and society, to that of being a selfish reason of feeling in love, the problems began to surface. Divorce began to become commonplace. Adultery, pre-marital sex, and many other problems became commonplace as well. Cohabiting became acceptable as an alternative to marriage. Now, as time has gone on, this progression has reached the point where people are willing to say that two men or two women who are in love should also be allowed to marry. All of this can be traced back to the change in the purpose of marriage.

I for one am ready to say that the line must be drawn here. It is high time not only to draw a line in the sand but to begin to push that line as far back into the enemy's camp as we can, taking back the ground that has been stolen from us. It is time that the living church of Jesus Christ rise up and begin taking dominion over the things in our country that we have allowed to fester for far too long. For too long have we left the definition of feminine beauty to Madison Avenue with their skinny bodies and flat, barren stomachs. In God's economy, real women have born children and have stretch marks! Historically, if a woman continued to have that pre-childbirth body, she was considered cursed, yet our society spends millions of dollars on plastic surgery and other products and procedures to try to get that form back. Our society praises what is cursed and curses what should be praised. If there is gross darkness in our society it is because there is no light in that situation. Scientifically speaking there is no such thing as darkness, only an absence of light. We need to be that light in our society. But we cannot be that light if we are confused about our stance on this subject. Not valuing children and family is at the root of many issues, including abortion, broken families, workaholism, homosexuality, and other alternate lifestyles.

We have spent a lot of time and resources trying to fight off the aforementioned societal problems to little avail. WHY? Because the people involved in those situations are confused by our selfish attitudes. They look at the church and say, "Hey, even you are limiting your children and expanding your careers because you want a nicer car, a nicer home, and you want to go on better vacations." Church, where is the separation from the world? How do we look different from our culture? I know that one way in which my family looks different is by having many children. Some people I work with look at me like

I just grew a second shrunken head on my shoulder when I tell them I have six children with another one on the way. I consider having a different life as part of my witness as a Christian. It's a very obvious way to show people that I'm not just living my life to collect toys and have fun, but instead am living for the eternal purposes of raising up a godly generation. Having a large family isn't easy, but nothing truly worthwhile in life is ever easy.

As we return to God's truths and begin to realize that this is a major doctrinal issue, we will see the miraculous provision of the Lord as we begin to take back all of things that the enemy has stolen from us in our country.

CHAPTER 8

Grab a Grand Vision from the Lord for Your Children

What if the Lord Blessed You with the Next Great Evangelist?

"Why bring children into such an evil world?... The children God gives us we will train to be leaders in this desperately sick world. Our children will... grow up to be the answer to many of the world's problems."
Rick and Jan Hess, A Full Quiver

What if Moses had been killed because the midwives didn't fear God and didn't know His plans and purposes for children? History would have been quite different, wouldn't it?

Do you know that the Lord has a grand vision for your life? He does, you know. You can see it when you read Scriptures such as these:

Jeremiah 1:5 — "Before I formed you in the womb I knew you; before you were born I sanctified you; I ordained you a prophet to the nations."

Psalm 22:10 — "I was cast upon You from birth. From My mother's womb You have been My God."

Psalm 139:13-16 — "For You formed my inward parts; You covered me in my mother's womb. I will praise You, for I am fearfully *and* wonderfully made; marvelous are Your works, and *that* my soul knows very well. My frame was not hidden from You, when I was made in secret, a*nd* skillfully wrought in the lowest parts of the earth. Your eyes saw my substance, being yet unformed. And in Your book they all were written, the days fashioned for me, when *as yet there were* none of them."

Isaiah 44:2 — "Thus says the Lord who made you and formed you from the womb, who will help you: 'Fear not, O Jacob My servant; And you, Jeshurun, whom I have chosen."

There are many others, of course, that speak of the Lord forming the child in the womb. God *personally* formed you in your mother's womb. That's a hard thing to get your mind around sometimes – that God, the Creator of the whole world, Designer of the entire universe, who has so many things on His mind and so many things on His "To Do List" — that this wonderful God took the time to form you as you grew in your mother's womb. It is an amazing thing.

God not only formed you in your mother's womb, but He also knew you from the beginning of time. He ordained your days before He created the world (Ps. 139:16). You have been "skillfully wrought" by God (Ps. 139:15) according to His plan for your life. God has a wonderful plan for you, He's known this plan all along, and He was preparing you for fulfilling this plan even before you were born.

And do you know what else? God has a grand plan for each of your children, just as He does for you. He has given each child the gifts, strengths, and abilities to fulfill His plan. Unfortunately, many people never reach their potential in life. As parents, there are many things we can do to help our children reach their potential. One of these things we can do is get a vision from the Lord of His plan for each of our children.

When we have God's vision for our children, we can use this to help us when making decisions for our children while they are young. For instance, if the Lord is showing you that your child will be a musician or worship leader, you can use this information to start the child in music lessons at the appropriate age. You can also use this information to relax if this child doesn't excel in math or science or sports. You know how the Lord has prepared your child's gifts and abilities, and you can rest in the knowledge that he or she is on the path God intends for them.

Another important reason to get God's vision for your child is that you need to teach this vision to the child. Your child needs to know that God has a plan for their life. They need to learn more about their specific plan as they grow. This understanding will protect them from many of the traps they will face in this fallen sinful world. A child who knows they are special in God's mind won't be as likely to react to peer pressure or strive to fit in during the teen years. A child who is certain of their goal won't be as likely to get sidetracked along the road of life with people and activities that distract them from this goal. A child that has a purpose to their life will be less likely to find themselves depressed, despondent, and aimless as so many teenagers and young adults are. A young person who knows God's plan for their life will make a wise choice when choosing a spouse, seeking one who will further their ministry rather than detract from it. Protect your child from these pitfalls – teach them that God has a wonderful plan for them, and help them discover what that plan is.

And please remember that the value of the child in God's eyes is totally separate from the circumstances of their conception. In Genesis 38, we read that Tamar got pregnant by Judah, her father-in-law, when she tricked him, and birthed the twins Perez and Zerah. Perez was in the lineage of Jesus. Also consider Solomon. His parents didn't get the most righteous start. King David committed sin with Bathsheba and then had her husband killed when she got pregnant. That child died when he was seven days old, but Solomon was their next child. He wasn't David's oldest child, but he was the one chosen by God to succeed him on the throne of Israel, and God blessed him more than any other king of Israel. So, regardless of whether your child was longed for by you or was a surprise, or whatever the circumstances, God knew exactly what He was doing when He created your child. Seek Him to learn His purpose for their life, and then do everything you can to help your child fulfill that purpose.

You can even pray for your children before they are born, as well as ask the Lord for children! What a novel thought. I know many parents who pray, *Lord please no more children*, but Hannah prayed that she would have a child, and even before he was born she dedicated him to the Lord to serve Him all the days of his life. That child was the prophet Samuel. How different Israel's history might have been had Hannah not asked for that child from the Lord. Samuel grew up to be a mighty prophet of the Lord, so much so that the Lord said He would not let one of Samuel's words fall to the ground, meaning everything the prophet spoke would surely come to pass.

Go ahead — let your imagination run wild! What if the Lord were to give you a child who might become the doctor who finds a cure for cancer? What if He gives you a future great scientist who finds a new clean burning fuel that will help clear pollution? Now I know what you are thinking. You are saying that I'm just having delusions of grandeur. To that I say that if I'm going to raise children for the Lord's service, why not raise children who are going to become grand champions in all they do? Maybe you or I will have children who will work diligently as janitors or greeters in the house of the Lord. May those children perform their God-given duties with all that is within them, knowing that when they step into eternity, only then will they see the impact that their seemingly insignificant ministry really had, with possibly tens of thousands of lives ultimately being touched by their ministry.

The bottom line is that I do not want to meet the Lord and have Him tell me that because of my selfishness I missed having a child who would have greatly impacted His creation had they been given a chance at life. I have too many regrets already; I really want to limit any more regrets I may have in the future. I have dear friends in the church who have a great vision for seeing powerful Christian leaders raised up and influencing political arenas; how sad it would be to get to heaven only to find out that this never happened because those children were never born. So in this area, as a couple, sit back and pray, spend time with the Lord, and imagine the things that could potentially be accomplished through your godly seed.

CHAPTER 9

Parents, Be Not as Little Children in the Lord

The Short Sheeting of Christian Maturity

"Children are the luxury of marital life, the treasure of the parents, the wealth of the family life. Their presence develops a great number of virtues in the parents, the father and mother—love, devotion, and self-sacrifice, the care for the future, interest in the community, the art of education. Children check selfishness in parents, reconcile the contrasts, soften the differences, bring the hearts of the parents ever closer to each other, give them a common interest that lives outside themselves, and opens their eyes and hearts to their surroundings and posterity. They

uphold to the parents, as if in mirrors, their own virtues and defects, force them to reconsider their lives, soften their criticisms, and teach them how difficult it is to rule a human being. Out of the family life there proceeds a reforming power toward the parents. Who recognizes in the sensible, industrious father of a family the boisterous youth of former days, and who ever suspected the light-hearted maid of being changed, through her first-born, into a mother who willingly makes supreme sacrifices with cheerful patience? Family life turns the selfish into servants, misers into heroes, coarse men into considerate fathers, and tender mothers into courageous fighters." Herman Bavinck, quoted by J. Norval Geldenhuys in **The Intimate Life.**

One of God's goals in our lives is to grow our faith. Hebrews 11:6 says, "But without faith [it is] impossible to please [God]." God wants our faith to grow, and He brings circumstances into our lives to accomplish this purpose. Having many children is one way to grow your faith.

When you have many children, it pushes you to rely on the Lord. Whether the pressure is financial, emotional, or physical, the answer is to turn to the Lord and have faith that He will meet whatever need you have. You must place yourself squarely in God's hands. What better place to be! What other place could be more secure? What other place could be safer? Being in our own hands? Certainly not! God knows all things, and He can do all things. He knew the future from before the beginning. Through faith, I can trust Him to do the right thing, for my good (and my children's). Through faith I can see miracles from His hand. Remember, if you are never in need of a miracle, you will never see one.

Many preachers have likened faith to a muscle – if you never use it, it won't grow. This has been true in my own life. With each child we have been forced to grow. We have grown in patience, faith, wisdom, and love. We have had to adjust our lives each time, but each of these adjustments has been a GOOD one. For instance, with each child, we spend less time watching TV. That's a good thing! Shannon is getting better at cooking from scratch instead of buying a box mix for dinner. It's much healthier to cook from scratch, and generally less expensive, so that's another good thing. We are getting better at setting our priorities; we are more organized with our time and energy. That's also a good thing! All of these things are things God wants to develop in His people, and He has used each new child to grow something new in us or to develop something further in our lives.

This same idea carries over into how we discipline our children. With our first child, we didn't need to do very much discipline when she was little. She was a very sweet, very compliant child (not perfect, of course, but easy-going by nature). It was a good thing too, since we were so young and inexperienced. God knows exactly what we need! As our second and third children came along, we realized that not all children are easy to train, so we began to search for answers and guidance. We searched the Scriptures, we read books on raising children, and we tried different approaches. Some approaches we liked, others we didn't. We began to develop our own style of discipline, and it has worked. And yet, with each new child, we still learned something new. As time has gone on, especially when our fifth child started crawling and exploring the house, we have realized that it's much easier to nip behavior in the bud at an early age rather than waiting until there is a real problem. What a revelation! So, as time goes on, we are becoming better parents. Praise God!

In doing research for this book, we realized how many great men and women of God were among the youngest in their families. For example, John and Charles Wesley were the last two children in their family. Benjamin Franklin was his father's fifteenth child. Joseph was Jacob's eleventh child. David was the youngest of seven. There are many others, including presidents, scientists, great composers and others who were all among the last children born to their parents. As we asked the Lord for the reason behind this, we realized that every parent gets better as they go. Parenting is on-the-job training – you can't read a book or take a class to learn everything there is to know before your first child is born. It doesn't work that way. So, naturally, parents get better as they go, and when they have many children, their younger children benefit from their parents' growth and the growth of the older children.

Not only do the parents grow and mature in large families, but the children do also. They have many more opportunities to learn to share and get along with other people, even from a young age. They learn to minister to others and to work together, simply because they are together so much. The older children learn how to take care of their younger siblings, which gives them a great head start for when they start their own families. The younger siblings can get their experience by babysitting their nieces and nephews. It all works together.

We really need to grasp this concept. Generally, as we have more children, we mature more. As we mature more in the Lord, we become more adept at training them. As we become more adept at training them, this will carry over into spiritual training. Think about this. If we can handle and effectively train many children, then the Lord knows that He can use us to train and disciple many spiritual children. Having more children will directly affect our desire and ability to effectively evangelize and disciple new believers. We believe this has been part of God's plan all along. When you have learned as a parent how to successfully disciple your natural children, you then will be more able to apply the same techniques and teaching to spiritual children. As parents, learning to disciple many children with many personalities prepares us to be able to disciple many spiritual children, especially ones that may come from difficult backgrounds, including those with ingrained habits and serious difficulties.

We believe that one of the reasons the Lord gives us children is so that we can hone our skills in parenting and discipleship. Our own children are a thousand times more forgiving and easier to deal with than most adults would be, allowing us to learn lessons in natural parenting that we can then translate into spiritual parenting. This is part of the Lord's natural progression - we learn how to do it with our own children and then carry those lessons over to new believers. Of course this is not the only way that God prepares people for being good spiritual parents. The Apostle Paul is a perfect example of this. He had no natural children, yet he was a spiritual father to many. He obviously learned the principles of discipleship in other ways, according to God's plan for his life. We are not saying that you can only become a good mentor if you have had many children. That's not true at all. Our point is that having many children is one way that God can use to prepare us to be spiritual parents. Regardless of the number of children God chooses to give us, we can trust that He will use them to help prepare us for other ministry. What a wonderful plan!

CHAPTER 10

Too Many Flowers?
The Joys of Parenting AND How to Enjoy Your Children

"The best thing I've ever done? Well, I've created four beautiful children. You mean, other than that?" Donald Trump, in Esquire

Parenting is full of joy. Yes, there are hardships and challenges, but in the end, there are many joys involved in molding these small people into the image of Christ. How else can you see the world through new eyes and rediscover simple things that you have taken for granted since you were small? Here are some examples of the joys we have experienced as parents.

When our oldest daughter, Tasha, was in kindergarten, she was already reading very well. She has always had a flair for drama, and this was demonstrated when she would read aloud. She made sure that her reading included the inflection, even going back to re-read a section if she wasn't satisfied with how loud or inquisitive-sounding it was when she read it the first time. At the time, I (Shannon) was working full time, so she went to day care for much of the day. One of her favorite things to do was sit down and read stories to the other younger children. Quite often when we would arrive to pick her up we'd have to wait for her to finish the story. It was so sweet to see the other children so happy to have her read stories to them. Even now she loves to read to her little sisters and brothers!

Our oldest son, Caleb, has always wanted to be just like Daddy. We have a cute picture of him at about age two, trying to wear Daddy's big black boots. They came up well over his knees! It was so cute to see him "walking" around like Daddy in those big black boots.

A couple of years later Caleb was memorizing 1 John 4:10 for a class at church. We have always had the children memorize the whole verse, not just part of it as they do in some of the younger classes. It was so sweet to hear him say "propitiation for our sins." He doesn't know what propitiation is yet, but he will someday. And whenever I read that verse, the memory of my sweet four-year-old son saying his verses will come back and bring tears to my eyes every time.

When Caleb was about three years old, he was doing something he knew he wasn't supposed to do.

When Daddy caught him in the act, he asked Caleb if he was "busted," our family's term for being in trouble. Caleb answered, "I'm not busted, I'm cute!" Jim had a hard time keeping a straight face for that one, and disciplined him anyway of course, but we still laugh about his "explanation."

Our second daughter, Cassie, at age four, was trying to play her favorite song, "Jesus Loves Me," on the piano. She has a cloth songbook of Christian children's songs, and it includes the music with the words. So, she sat down at the piano to play her songs with her music, as she has seen many of us do. It was so sweet to hear her singing along with her piano playing. Her singing was good, but she's never had any piano lessons so she was just hitting random notes. It was precious!

When Caleb and Cassie pretend play, they love to act out things they have seen. They will act out movies or TV shows they have seen, or sometimes stories we have read them or even the video games they like to play. When they are doing this pretend play, they call it "playing with our skins." I don't know where they came up with it, but it's very cute to hear them talking about pretending to be Dora the Explorer saving baby Jaguar "with their skins."

Our second son, Jace, was still learning to talk, and that is always a precious time. He had been learning "his" song. Several of our children have a song that goes with their name, something silly that we have made up. It's just a fun way to sing about the child (or to them), and it's especially nice when they are two years old and you have been saying their name all day with a negative tone of voice. Jace's song is the old Batman song; only instead of "Batman!" we say, "Jace-man!" Jace started to sing along: "Na-na-na Jace-man!" (He didn't get all the syllables in there yet!) It was so cute, and he loved to sing it with you.

Jace is my little worshipper, though. Even from a young age, he would raise his hands in church when he saw Daddy raising his hands, and he loved to clap when everyone else did. The other night we were having a worship time at home and he was singing along with some of the songs, raising his hands, clapping and dancing. It's precious.

Our third son, Zachary, is my helper, and my engineer. He's the cleverest child at figuring out mechanical things. He shocked me at eighteen months old when he started opening the cupboards that had childproof locks on them. Yikes! It's delightful to watch him with a new toy, though. He is so intent on learning all about how it works, and he will sit and play with it for a very long time. You can see the gears working in his mind as he learns. It will be so much fun to do science with him in school!

Zachary has always been fascinated with our cat. He just loves to watch him and, of course, try to touch him. Since the petting of a fifteen-month-old wasn't exactly gentle, I've had to work with him to teach him how to pet kitty the right way. Zach would squeal with delight as I helped him pet kitty, then he gets overwhelmed and just has to try to eat those cool ears or grab a fistful of fur. Our cat is pretty good-natured toward our children, but even he has his limits, so I would have to move Zach and get him involved in something else before he pushed kitty too far. Zach has learned, though, and he's eventually figure out how to pet kitty nicely. Kitty was very happy when that day came!

Our fourth son, Kyran, is now fourteen months old. He's always been all smiles, all the time. Everywhere we go, if we take Kyran, we have to leave extra time in the schedule because people love to stop and talk to him. He always smiles at everyone, young and old. He has a magnetic personality that draws people to him. I can't wait to see what the Lord uses that for in the future!

There are several joys in parenting that I haven't experienced yet, but I expect to someday. I expect to enjoy helping my children choose a spouse and get married. I expect to have grandchildren (lots of them!) and great-grandchildren. I pray that I will have the peace of seeing each of my children (and grandchildren, and great-grandchildren) accept the Lord and serve Him with all their heart. I look forward to seeing the wonderful things the Lord has planned for them, and I look forward to having the opportunity to cover them in prayer, even when they don't know they need it. I pray that someday when I am old and gray I won't be left in a nursing home, alone and lonely. I pray that I will be able to grow old and eventually pass on to see the Lord, while surrounded by my family, loved and cared for. Life is good!

I know many of you are thinking that your children don't bring you very much joy. Instead they bring you stress and trouble. I'm sure some of you would say that you don't want to spend much time with your children; you might even deliberately avoid spending time with them because it is such a trial. Take heart! There is hope! Your children can be trained, and once they are trained they will bring you joy and be a testimony of God's goodness.

There is a very important principle to remember about raising children. You must remember that each of your children is a sinner. They were born that way. They will either fight against the flesh or give into it for the rest of their lives. Either way, they cannot avoid the effect of sin. They may be beautiful and look very innocent when they are born, but it doesn't take long for sin and self to show up in their behavior. I have never doubted the fact that we are born in sin, especially since the first time my two-year-old child stamped his foot and told Jim "NO!" Children don't realize that resisting in this way can risk their life. Most adults outweigh a two-year-old by many times and could do serious damage to them if they chose to. Yet small children still try to manifest their own will against such incredible odds. It's in their nature to do this; they can't help it.

However, they can *learn* to behave differently. Any child, even very, very young children, can learn different behavior based on the response they get from the environment around them. A child who touches something hot probably won't touch it again. They can learn, and they can change their behavior when it suits them. The key to training your children is to make good behavior more pleasant than bad behavior. We humans are naturally lazy and prefer to take the easy way out. When we realize that proper behavior is the easy way, because bad behavior gets us punished or is otherwise uncomfortable (like burning our finger on the stove), we will usually choose the good behavior, because it's easier.

So I have two general principles that I follow when training my children. The first is that they NEVER get what they want when they misbehave. If you let them have what they were trying to get by using improper methods (whining, sneaking, etc) then they will learn that the misbehavior works and they will use it again. So, even if I was going to give that thing to the child, I won't when they misbehave to get it. The second principle is that I have to make the child uncomfortable with their misbehavior. If I am the only one upset by the behavior, it won't change. The child must feel uncomfortable with their misbehavior, and only then will the behavior change. These two principles can be applied to just about any child-training situation to guide you to a solution.

I would also like to mention two other important points that are vital when it comes to training children. The first is that we must pray for them, and when we come across a difficult situation, we need to pray and ask the Lord for guidance in responding to it properly. I have seen amazing results just from praying for my children about a situation. Sometimes I get guidance from the Lord about how to respond. Sometimes the situation is resolved in another way aside from anything I do. God is amazing, and prayer really works!

The second important point is that the earlier you start to adjust your child's behavior, the easier it will be. When I (Shannon) was a younger mother, I would ignore things in my children even though they bothered me. I would consider certain bad behaviors to be "just a phase," or I would think the children were too young to know better, so I would ignore the behavior. But the problems didn't go away – they grew as the child grew. They went from a brief annoyance to an ingrained habit, and changing the behavior went from addressing it a couple of times to digging in my heels and having to be vigilant for weeks or months to change those habits. For example, I used to wait until the child was older, maybe two or three, before I would expect them to understand that they shouldn't play with items on coffee tables in another person's house. I was convinced that the child couldn't understand until that age, and since it was such a pain to fight with a one-year-old over the issue, we just didn't go to people's houses.

Then I realized that I could teach my crawling baby not to touch things that were dangerous, like power cords and such. One day I realized that my baby could learn to NOT touch dangerous things at that age because I worked with them in order to teach them this. So why not try to teach them to NOT touch other things that were annoying but not especially dangerous? So, I tried it with the power button on the TV. Our TV has a beautiful red light right next to the power button, and this is located at just the right height for a baby who is learning to stand, so our children have all played with the light and accidentally turned the TV off, then on, then off, and then on again. You get the picture. It was much more fun for them because they got such a reaction from whoever was watching the TV at the time they turned it off, so they learned very quickly how to become the center of attention in this manner.

I decided to try to teach my baby to NOT touch the TV. I used the same method that I used with dangerous things. I would swat their hand and tell them "No" each time they would touch the object. This baby had already learned what No means, so it didn't take very long to learn to leave the TV power button alone. I was very excited. This baby learned to NOT touch all sorts of things – the dog food and water, my glasses, the toilet paper, the cat. He was such a well-behaved baby. My friends all wanted a baby as content as he was. I realized that there was a side benefit of this training I'd been doing. My baby was now good enough at obeying "No" that I could tell him "No" to something new and he would simply obey. I could even tell him "No" from across the room and he would stop reaching for the thing and go play with something else, at least most of the time. This was my one-year-old baby, mind you. I was so happy! So, don't wait until these things become a huge habitual issue. Handle them while the child is small and it will only take a small correction.

I know that many people get upset at the thought of "spanking" a baby. Please understand that I'm not talking about taking a paddle to a small child. I'm talking about a swat on the hand, preferably the hand that was touching the object that is off limits. And I'm only talking about a swat hard enough to sting and get the baby's attention, which is not being abusive.

Don't be angry or yell at the baby. Be calm but firm and the child will learn what you expect. Children can behave how they are expected to behave. You teach your children your expectations through your actions and your reactions to what they do.

For those of you who have older children, don't despair. You can still train your children. It's just harder if you wait longer, and you have to be more diligent and more consistent. Start by repenting before the Lord for your previous mistakes, and then ask Him to help you change YOUR behavior. Once your behavior changes, your children will change too. Then choose one or two areas that need to be addressed first. If the children are old enough to understand, explain the new rules to them and outline the consequences of breaking the rules. Then, expect them to test you, because they will, and make sure you respond as you said you would. Once your children are sure you mean business, they will adjust their behavior pretty quickly. The key is consistency. If you would like more information, we have included a very helpful website in the Resources section that tells the story of how one mom re-trained her children when they were older.

Also, please remember that children are still children. They still need to act like children, not like small adults. They still don't have the experience to know what you know, so they will still make childish mistakes and act foolishly. Don't expect so much of your children that they never get to act like children. We need to have balance between expecting our children to behave properly and letting them run and play like children. Prayer will help you discern this balance in your family for your children.

There is far more that could be said about training children. The situations we face as parents are endless. And each child is different, so just when you think you've figured it out, one of your children will be different than the rest and present you with a new situation. This information should give you a good start. If you are interested in further reading or study, I recommend a study of the book of Proverbs. God has given us many principles of child rearing in the Bible, and many of them are in Proverbs. We have also listed our favorite child training resources in the Resources section at the end of this book.

Don't be afraid to train your children. They will be happier, and so will you, and you will experience the joy of parenting as God intends for you.

CHAPTER 11

Don't Fear the Unknown
In Mathematical Terms,
Let the Lord Solve for "X"

"Women should not have children after 35. Thirty-five children are enough." - Anonymous

I n this book, we have looked at the issue of reproductive rights from a scriptural perspective. We
have studied scriptures that clearly outline how God
desires for His children to "be fruitful and multiply."
We have discovered that God considers children to
be a blessing and a reward. We have also learned
that God is the One who opens and closes the womb.
Without God's direct involvement, conception
doesn't happen.

The purpose for pointing out these scriptures
is to say that reproductive rights belong to no one

but the Lord. We as Christians are always talking about how we should be surrendering our lives to His control, yet in this one area in modern society we refuse to relinquish control, when clearly God wants to raise up in His children a godly, eternal heritage. I know fellow Christians who spend much time in prayer discerning the Lord's will for a specific situation in their life, but when it comes to having children, they believe "this is OUR decision." This mindset is totally inconsistent with Scripture.

We have analyzed each of the various forms of birth control available to couples today. We have seen how most of these can be physically damaging to husband or wife. We have seen how many of these forms of birth control are abortifacient, and that women who have been using them may sadly find many more of their own children in heaven than they expected to see. We have seen that there is only one option that is NOT physically damaging (NFP), but many still consider it to be unsound scripturally. We have also seen that birth control was NOT embraced by any church denomination until the 1930s. I don't think it is a coincidence that major societal changes happened in our country, and are still happening, within a generation of that change in belief. It would seem that we are reaping the harvest of allowing the world to influence the church toward satisfying self and the flesh instead of working to have the church influence the world toward godliness and faith.

We have discussed the difference Christians could make in our society by embracing large families. We have compared the legacy left by a family where every generation has two children to that of a family where every generation has five children. The difference is staggering! On that basis alone, we could see a total change in the spiritual, social, and political climate in our country. This would be truly "confronting our enemy in the gates."

We have talked about how having many children helps us to grow in our faith and walk with the Lord. We have seen that when we have many children, we are forced to become more full of faith, to grow out of our immaturity, to embrace the work of the Lord in our lives, and to believe Him for miracles that proclaim His power and glory to everyone around us. All of these things are goals the Lord has for our lives anyway.

We have talked about how God has a grand vision for each child He gives life to. We have seen that it is our duty as parents to seek the Lord and discover this vision for our children so we can help them accomplish their life's calling. What a privilege to partner with God and our children to accomplish something wonderful!

We have also talked about the joys that come with parenting. Some of these joys are small ones, like the first kiss from your toddler or when your child brings you a dandelion bouquet. Some of these are great big joys, like when your child gets married to just the right person or has their first child or when they give their heart to the Lord. When we enjoy our children on a daily basis, parenting is a joy, not a chore.

With all of this in mind, we must ask ourselves a very important question. If God has planned every person from before He created the world, what risks are we taking if we attempt to control conception? We must ask ourselves how we could presume to know better than God on this subject. I (Shannon) have tried to live my life so I wouldn't regret my actions. I have plenty of regret in my life, just as we all do, but I try to live so that I won't look back and feel regret because I knew better than to do something but did it anyway. For instance, I try to treasure those nights spent cuddling my babies while they nurse because I know they will grow up fast enough and I don't want to regret missing out on those cuddles. With regard to having children, one of the big reasons I have chosen to allow God to control when and how many children we have is because I don't want any more regret in that area. (I already regret waiting 9 years between our first and second children, and I sometimes wonder what delightful people might have been born during those years.) I don't want to stand before the Lord and have Him tell me that I would have birthed the next Beethoven or Galileo or Moody or Da Vinci, if only I'd allowed Him to give me one more (or two more or three more or however many more) children. What regret that would be, to find out that God had planned something tremendous, but that our own actions hindered His plan.

So, consider well what you will do with this information. Seek the Lord for confirmation about what to do in your own life.

CHAPTER 12

Now What?
My Husband/Wife Thinks I'm Crazy!

"When you get married, the Bible says that the two people become one flesh. Life sure would be easier if you became one brain, too." - Jim and Shannon French

In writing this book, the last thing we want to do is add any stress to the relationship between a husband and wife. The good Lord knows that there are already sufficient ways in which we stress our marriages. It is, however, important for both husband and wife to always strive for unity and harmony. We also know that in any marriage there will be points of contention and disagreement from time to time.

If after reading this book, you and your spouse disagree on this issue, you need to pray that much more, until you come to unity on the issue as a couple. This is far too important an issue for you to accept differing opinions. Continue praying, and then continue praying some more until you come to agreement. Do not allow stubbornness, pride, complacency, or the enemy to drive a wedge between you and your spouse. You should pray together, seek the Lord's face, ask Him to change your own heart first to align with His, and then pray for understanding. Seek the wisdom of Scripture and godly counsel from those you trust who have a firm grasp of the truth of God's Word. ALWAYS be respectful of each other and sincerely try to understand your spouse's point of view. Also, do not be too hasty to rush a process that the Lord may be completing in one or both of you. Our experience has been (and I'm quite sure it will remain this way) that neither one of us has yet achieved our ultimate sanctification. Each of us is a work in progress.

We can tell you that it is possible to have unity and harmony on even very tough issues. The price of unity is eternal vigilance and lots of patience. You must guard your hearts and minds at all times and allow the Lord to change you fully into all that He has destined for you to be. And you must be patient and allow the Lord to do the same in your husband or wife.

If you are a wife who wants to be Quiver^x but your husband doesn't agree, you need to combine submission with wisdom and prayer. First, continue to pray that the Lord will bring you and your husband into unity of opinion on the subject. Second, ask the Lord to give you wisdom about how to submit to your husband's authority without violating your conscience and convictions. Also ask Him for wisdom in explaining your opinion to your husband in a clear yet submissive way. For instance, if your husband wanted you to use hormonal birth control and you felt that was unacceptable, you should ask the Lord about how to make a godly appeal to your husband about why you don't feel comfortable with that birth control method, and perhaps concede to use a different method, like NFP, out of submission to your husband's decision. But most of all do everything you can to remain respectfully in submission to your husband, even if you disagree with his decision. If you don't, you could be opening a Pandora's box of trouble in your marriage. For instance, if you ignored your husband's desire for using birth control and did get pregnant, your marriage could be seriously damaged, and likely so would the relationship between your husband and that child. Continue to pray, and be patient.

If you are a husband who wants to be Quiver^x and your wife doesn't agree, please be patient and pray for her. Remember that some women find pregnancy and childbirth more difficult than others do, and perhaps that is one reason your wife hesitates. Or perhaps she has other reasons on her mind. Trying to discuss the issue with her will help you understand why she disagrees with you. Much of the work in living a Quiver^x life falls to the wife and mother, so listen carefully to her concerns. You may find that some of her concerns are things you can help with, and some of them may be things you can't help with. Help with the things you can, and pray that the Lord will change her heart about the rest. If you try to pressure her into agreement, she will probably resent it and that will cause all sorts of problems in your marriage. Be patient and let the Lord work. He is faithful!

In the end, be sure you both have a clear conscience before the Lord in this area. Don't ignore the issue and get to a point later in your life where you regret your decisions. Spend the time to seek the Lord and invest yourself in what the Lord would have you to do. The rewards gained from obeying the Lord are well worth the effort.

Resources

Good explanation of hormonal birth control side effects - http://mercola.com/2004/jun/12/contraception_facts.htm

Many quotes regarding the consequences of low birth rates in Europe and Israel - http://www.telegraph.co.uk/opinion/main.jhtml;$sessionid$NI4VWCWKTWMV3QFIQMGSFFWAVCBQWIV0?xml=/opinion/2003/12/23/do2302.xml&sSheet=/opinion/2003/12/23/ixopinion.html

Crown Financial Ministries
Vision: To see the followers of Christ in every nation faithfully living by God's financial principles in every area of their lives. We particularly like their Money Matters Software ($60).
www.crown.org; (800) 722-1976; P.O. Box 100, Gainesville, GA 30503-0100

The Woodshed – a website written by a mother of ten children who began to re-train her children when she had 3 children, ages six, four, and two. Very inspirational!
http://www.atriptothewoodshed.com/

No Greater Joy Ministries –
Michael and Debi Pearl
Authors of *To Train Up A Child, No Greater Joy,* vol. 1-3, and other books. We found these books to be very enlightening regarding child training.
http://www.nogreaterjoy.org/; 1000 Pearl Road, Pleasantville TN 37033

Affirmative Parenting - John Rosemond
He is the author of several books on parenting. I don't agree with everything he has to say, but I have gleaned lots of insight and several creative ideas from reading his articles on his website.
http://www.rosemond.com/

Buying coupons online
http://www.dabsforms.com/Shop/
(Shannon's favorite)
http://www.couponsandforms.com/

Other Quotes on the Subject

"Many people have said to me, 'What a pity you had such a big family to raise. Think of the novels and the short stories and the poems you never had the time to write because of that.' And I looked at my children and I said, 'These are my poems. These are my short stories.'" - Olga Masters, Australian Writer (1919-1986)

"...[A]s Judæo-Christian tradition has always insisted, "wasting the seed" by intrinsically sterile types of genital action violates that *natural* law to which all men, Jew and Gentile alike, have always had access by virtue of their very humanness, (cf. Rom. 1:26-27; 2:14), this will explain perfectly why Onan's sexual action *in itself* would be presented in Scripture as meriting a most severe divine judgment: it was a perverted act - one of life-suppressing lust. Indeed, over and above its prohibition by natural law, such deliberately sterilized pleasure-seeking could well have been discerned as a form of contravening one of the few divine precepts which already in that pre-Sinai tradition had been solemnly revealed - and repeated - in positive, verbal form: "Increase and multiply" (Gen. 1:27-28; 9:1)." Harrison, Rev. Brian W. (1996 November). The Sin of Onan Revisited [Electronic Version]. *Living Tradition, Organ Of The Roman Theological Forum, No. 67*. Retrieved December 3, 2004 from http://www.rtforum.org/lt/lt67.html

"By profession, I am a soldier and take great pride in that fact. But I am prouder, infinitely prouder, to be a father. ...It is my hope that my son, when I am gone, will remember me not from the battle, but in the home, repeating with him the simple prayer, 'Our Father, which art in heaven.'" General Douglas MacArthur, 1942

"Hence note, 'tis one of the greatest outward blessings to have a family full of dutiful children. To have many children is the next blessing to much grace. To have many children about us is better than to have much wealth about us. To have store of these olive plants (as the Psalmist calls them) round about our table is better than to have store of oil and wine upon our table. We know the worth of dead, or rather, lifeless treasures, but who knows the worth of living treasures? ...But though all things are of God, yet all things are not alike of him: children are more of God than houses or lands." David Caryl, quoted in Spurgeon's *Treasury of David*.

"In marriage, as the marriage law declares, the man and woman come together for the procreation of children. Therefore, whoever makes the procreation of children a greater sin than copulation, forbids marriage and makes the woman not a wife but a mistress, who for some gifts presented to her is joined to the man to gratify his passion." Augustine, 354-430, *The Morals of the Manichees, http://www.valerieslivingbooks.com/history.htm*

"To have coitus other than to procreate children is to do injury to nature." Clement of Alexandria,?-215, *The Instructor, Paedagogus, http://www.valeriesliv-ingbooks.com/history.htm*

"Two things a pastor should impress upon married people: 1. that God would bless their marriage with children; 2. that God holds parents responsible for the Christian training of their children. A husband and wife should according to God's will become the father and the mother of children. One of God's purposes of marriage is the propagation of the human race. God says: "Be fruitful and multiply and replenish the earth" (Gen. 1:28; Ps. 127 and 128; Fourth Commandment). A Hebrew married woman considered it an affliction to be childless (1 Sam. 1:1-20). The Jews had large families; so did our German forefathers. The one-, two-, or three-children family system is contrary to the Scriptures; for man has no right arbitrarily or definitely to limit the number of his offspring (birth control), especially not if done with artificial or unnatural means (Gen. 1:28; Ps. 127:3-

6; Ps. 128:3-4; Gen. 38:9-10). Such restrictions as uncontrollable circumstances, natural barrenness, or the ill health of wife or husband put upon the number of offspring are the exceptions to the rule. Child-bearing is both a natural and healthful process, while any interference with natural functions is injurious." Fritz, John H. C., 1874-1953 http://www.valerieslivingbooks.com/history.htm

"Because God's favor appears in no outward thing more than in the increase of children, he promises to enrich the faithful with this gift." *Geneva Bible Notes*, on Psalm 128:3 (1599) http://www.valerieslivingbooks.com/history.htm

1. It is sinful.
   A. It is willfully setting aside God's will and command (Gen. 1:28; 1 Tim. 5:14; 2:15; Gen. 38:9, 10).
   B. It is despising His promises and is depriving oneself of a blessing (Ps. 127 and 128).
   C. It is usurping for oneself an exclusive privilege of God, that of giving or withholding children (Ps. 127:3; Gen. 29:31-30:6; 30:22; 33:5; 16:2; 20:18; Lev. 20:20-21; Job 42:12-13; Luke 1:58; 1 Sam. 1:10-11).
   D. Birth control by the means of anticonceptuals, coitus interruptus, etc., is ruthlessly interfering with God's method of creating a living being. Hufeland, one of the most noted physicians of Germany, 1762-1836, says, 'The first question undoubtedly is, "When

does life begin?" There can be no doubt that the act of copulation is to be regarded as the beginning of the existence of the future being and that the very first, even though invisible, germ of his being has the developed man ... A human being is being murdered in his incipiency. I am not going to answer sophistic, even Jesuitic, cavils. I appeal to sane reason and to the pure, unspoiled moral feeling of every man ... The product presupposes producing, and if it is wrong to kill the product, then it goes without saying that it is wrong to render futile the act whereby it is being produced, for thereby is its first beginning.' This is undoubtedly the Scriptural view. Cf. Ps. 139:13-16; Job 10:8-11, especially v. 10 (the act of copulation described).

E. Marriage degenerates from a holy estate to mere gratification of carnal lust (Heb. 13:4; I Thess. 4:4).

2. It undermines the State. It is race suicide. Even the two-children system will rapidly lead to extermination of a people, for ten percent of all marriages are naturally childless, and unmarried people do not contribute to the growth of a nation, while the two-children system replaces only the parents...hence a decrease in population, and the nation will die out. At least four children to a family [are needed] to prevent this dying out [process]; five children to bring about an increase in population.

3. It undermines the home. Parents become selfish, incompatible. Children [become] idolized, pampered, egotistic, self-important, undesirable citizens in many instances. A Supreme Court Justice is quoted as saying: 'It is my conclusion that childless homes are responsible for the almost complete absence of real home-life. I cannot help but reach the conclusion that, if our women had children, there would be more happiness and fewer divorces. Presence of children attracts the husband to his home and keeps the mothers from the gossiping neighbors and bridge parties. Absence of children promotes discord. Their presence makes for harmony.'" Laetsch, Theodore F. K., 1877-1962, "Arguments Against Birth Control" http://www.valerieslivingbooks.com/history.htm

"In spite of extended argument not a single passage can be adduced from Scripture which in any remote way condones birth control; and no one acquainted with the Bible should hesitate to admit that it is a definite departure from the requirements of Scripture." Maier, Walter Arthur, 1893-1950, "The Blight of Birth Control" http://www.valerieslivingbooks.com/history.htm

"When home ties are loosened, when men and women cease to regard a worthy family life, with all its duties fully performed and all its responsibilities lived up to, as the best life worth living, then evil days for the commonwealth are at hand. There are regions in our land, and classes of our population, where the birth rate has sunk below the death rate. Surely it should need no demonstration to show that willful sterility is, from the standpoint of the human race, the one sin for which the national penalty is national death, race death—a sin for which there is no atonement." Roosevelt, Theodore Sixth Annual Message to Congress http://www.valeriesliving-books.com/history.htm

"Had the Pilgrim fathers and mothers disregarded the multiplication precept hurled from the eternal throne, at the dawn of man, into an unpeopled world, who would have thrown the tea of the oppressor into the ocean of liberty, who would have fought the colonial battles, whence would have come the three millions of unconquerable men and women, who would have rocked the cradle of liberty in which reposed an infant republic, and who would have guarded and nurtured that infant to a stately manhood, represented in 'Uncle Sam,' who now proclaims to the world that he rules the greatest nation, the most versatile people and the best governed republic that the sun has ever smiled on since thrown into space from the majestic hand of God? .... When Babylon, Sparta, Greece, Rome, and many other nations which have long since perished from the earth, had attained the zenith of their great-ness and culture, they sought the widest possible sexual liberality, but set bounds to their offspring, and willfully permitted their children to die or be eaten by beasts, thus unwittingly sapping their manhood and womanhood, and numerically weakening their nationality by ill attention to progeny, thereby hastening the approaching day when they were to lay the crown of centuries of glory in the lap of the invader." Sexton, M. H. *Matrimony Minus Maternity* http://www.valerieslivingbooks.com/history.htm

Notes

Chapter 2

1. On American Motherhood, by Theodore Roosevelt - A speech given by President Roosevelt in Washington on March 13, 1905, before the National Congress of Mothers
2. http://www.biblicalresearch.info/page56.html

Chapter 4

1. http://www.valerieslivingbooks.com/history.htm
2. http://www.ccel.org/fathers2/NPNF1-11/npnf1-11-88.htm#P3114_2910132
3. http://www.valerieslivingbooks.com/history.htm

4. http://www.valerieslivingbooks.com/ history.htm

5. http://www.valerieslivingbooks.com/ history.htm

6. http://www.pfli.org/endometrium_wilks. html

7. Dr. Chris Kahlenborn, MD, http://www. pfli.org/Kahlenborn_OCs.txt

8. http://www.pfli.org/Kahlenborn_OCs.txt

9. American College of Surgeons' Commission on Cancer study

10. Thorogood, M., Vessey, M., (1990). An epidemiologic survey of cardiovascular disease in women taking oral contraceptives. *Am J. Obsete Gynecol* 163 (1) pt 2, 274-281

11. http://www.pfli.org/pill_drug_nutrient_ depletions_duplantis.html

12. http://www.fda.gov/bbs/topics/ ANSWERS/2004/ANS01325.html FDA Talk Paper T04-50, November 17, 2004

13. http://www.guardian.co.uk/medicine/ story/0,11381,1492378,00.html

14. http://www.pfli.org/pill_drug_nutrient_ depletions_duplantis.html

15. *The Cincinnati Enquirer*, 24 Nov 1983, E-2. The newspaper story reported an article in a current issue of *Family Planning Perspectives*, a Planned Parenthood publication

16. Hershel Kick, A.M. Walker, et al., "Vaginal spermicides and the congenital disorders," *JAMA* 245:13 (3 Apr 1981) 1329-1332

17. William Booth, "Pregnancy disorder tied to condoms, diaphragms," *Washington Post* (8 Dec 1989) A-3. Reports on the work of Hillary Klonoff-Cohen described in *JAMA*, 8 Dec 1989.

18. http://scc.uchicago.edu/nonoxynol9.html

19. Germaine Greer, *Sex and Destiny: The Politics of Human Fertility* (New York: Harper and Row, 1984), p 193-195, 197, 199.

20. N.J. Alexander, and T. B. Clarkson, "Vasectomy increases the severity of diet-induced atherosclerosis in *Macacafasciularis*," *Science* (1978) 201:538-541

21. L. Rosenberg, J. R. Palmer, A. G. Zauber, et al., "Vasectomy and the risk of prostate cancer," *American Journal of Epidemiology* (1990) 132:1051-1055.

22. C. Mettlin, N. Natarajan, and P. Huben, "Vasectomy and prostate cancer risk," *American Journal of Epidemiology* (1990) 132:1056-1061.

23. E. Giovannucci, a. Ascherio, E. B. Rimm, et al, "A prospective cohort study of vasectomy and prostate cancer in U.S. men," *Journal of the American Medical Association* (1993) 269:873-877; E. Giovanucci, T. D. Tosteson, F. E. Speizer,

et al., " A retrospective cohort study of vasectomy and prostate cancer in U. S. men," *Journal of the American Medical Association* (1993) 269: 878-882.

24. http://dontfixit.org/forum/posts/063002.asp

25. Being Fruitful: A Biblical View of Birth Control, Patriarch Magazine, 7-31-01 http://www.patriarch.com/article.php?sid=94

26. William F. Colliton, Jr., M.D., FACOG, Birth Control Pill: Abortifacient and Contraceptive, available on-line at: http://www.epm.org/26doctor.html

27. Mother Teresa, An address at the National Prayer Breakfast (Sponsored by the U.S. Senate and House of Representatives) February 3, 1994

Chapter 5

1. The Boston Globe 2/22/04, Carlene Hempel, http://www.boston.com/news/globe/magazine/articles/2004/02/22/no_kids_please/

Chapter 7

1. http://www.catholic.com/library/Birth_Control.asp

Printed in the United States
51848LVS00003B/1-102

9 781600 340031